東
門

The Eastern Gate

An Invitation to the Arts of China and Japan

Shen Chou *Three Gardeners in A Fenced Enclosure*

JANET GAYLORD MOORE

The Eastern Gate

An Invitation to the Arts of China and Japan

COLLINS

Published by William Collins Publishers, Inc.,
Cleveland and New York, 1979.

Library of Congress Cataloging in Publication Data
Moore, Janet Gaylord.   The Eastern Gate.
SUMMARY: An illustrated introduction to the sculpture,
painting, and architecture of China and Japan.
1. Art, Chinese—Juvenile literature.
2. Art, Japanese—Juvenile literature.
[1. Art, Chinese. 2. Art, Japanese]   I. Title.
N7337.M66   709'.51   78-59816
ISBN 0-529-05434-5

The jacket illustration is a reproduction of Horse Race at the Kamo
Shrine *(artist unknown). One of a pair of six-fold screens, ink and color on gold ground paper.
The Cleveland Museum of Art, Purchase from the J.H. Wade Fund.*

For specific permissions and copyright information see also pages 251-255.

Acknowledgments

The writer would like to express her thanks to friends at The Cleveland Museum of Art, especially to members of the Department of Art History and Education for many courtesies: to Gabriel P. Weisberg, Curator; to James A. Birch; Adele Z. Silver; Marjorie Williams; and to Martin Linsey, not only for the photographs in this book, but for what he has taught me about the camera. My thanks go also to the staff of the Library for their long Patience, and to Nicholas Hlobeczy, in charge of the Photographic Studio, for many photographs. A special word of appreciation goes to members and former members of the Oriental Department staff: to Jean K. Cassill; Eleanor Pearlstein; and Nora Ling-yun Liu; to Henry Kleinhenz, for help when it was most needed; and to Margaret F. Marcus, for encouragement over the years. I am indebted to Norma Roberts for her care in the preparation of the manuscript.

Wai-kam Ho, Curator of Chinese Art, and Sherman E. Lee, Chief Curator of Oriental Art, have provided many learning opportunities in that remarkable teaching institution, The Cleveland Museum of Art. Dr. Lee, who is also Director of the Museum, has cheerfully read these chapters, but the plan of the book and any errors of fact or interpretation are my own. Finally I wish to express my gratitude to Iwao Setsu, of Tokyo, for help with photographs; to Dr. Beatrix von Ragué for opening doors for me in Japan and at the *Museum für Ostasiatsche Kunst* in Berlin; to the late Ogata Sohaku and his wife for guidance and hospitality at Chotoku-in of Shokoku-ji in Kyoto; and to Dr. and Mrs. Y. C. James Yen for never-to-be-forgotten kindness in Ting Hsien and Peking.

For
ELLIE
and in loving memory of her mother,
Catherine S. Auchincloss,
who opened for me
the gateway to the East

CONTENTS

Color Illustrations

Foreword

World War II was a true watershed in the understanding of the East by the West. The language barrier was breached for both China and Japan by the thousands of students needed by the armed forces, the diplomatic and economic missions, and then, after the war, by the work of reconstituting the ravaged areas of the Far East. But the new enlarged understanding was still quite imperfect as the Vietnam war so dramatically and tragically proved. Understanding comes in fits and starts, advances here and lags there.

A sympathetic knowledge of Far Eastern art is an essential part of our general understanding, for in both China and Japan, but particularly now in the latter, the arts are far more an integral part of all levels of culture than they are in most Western cultures, including the United

States. Specialized studies for the already interested student or the enthusiastic layman are reasonably numerous. But few such books can be confidently used by younger people or beginning laymen. For this audience *The Eastern Gate* should be at once both useful and delightful.

Janet Moore is an ideal author for this task. An accomplished artist and extremely effective and successful educator, she has lived in Peking and traveled extensively in China and Japan. She sees Far Eastern art in many ways—as an artist, a historian, a teacher, a student of nature—and these various ways make it possible for the insights of her text and selection of illustrations to intrigue and convince different readers with equally varied interests. While a few historians of Western art are aware of some indispensable contributions made by Eastern art, more scholars, teachers, and students should be aware of the implications for educational practice of such key subjects as those treated in the chapters titled "Chinese Writing: The Image of Thought," and "Zen, Sesshu, and the Way of Tea." The application of the underlying aesthetic and psychological processes suggested there—not to be confused with mere outward appearances—could have a profound effect on our poorly diffused and sadly deficient aesthetic mores.

Pleasure is not forbidden by such serious matters, and this book has an even greater measure of delight than of instruction. Why else would one make an effort to learn a foreign tongue, to understand a strange but fascinating art? The eighteenth-century philosophers were beguiled by their visions of Cathay. The artists and connoisseurs of the late nineteenth century were visually overwhelmed by what they perceived as the aesthetics of *Japonisme.* Now it is high time that we understood far more than these fashions, for the Orient is with us today more than ever before. Knowledge and accompanying delight are the rewards of what must be a continuing effort.

—Sherman E. Lee
Director, The Cleveland Museum of Art

To the Reader

One of the poems in the oldest collection of Chinese verse, *The Book of Songs,* begins:

> At the great gate to the East
> mid crowds
> be girls like clouds
> who cloud not my thought in the least.[1]

Anyone who has traveled in China or Japan in our own time remembers the gates—medieval gates of walled cities, imposing gates of palaces and temples, the modest but inviting gate of a house, an inn, or a shop. One recalls the massive main gate of the Forbidden City in Peking, adorned now with a huge portrait of Chairman Mao, or in Japan one thinks of the Torii—traditional gateway of a Shinto shrine, classic in its simple wooden construction, usually painted lacquer red, but sometimes revealing the color and grain of the natural wood.

Some people find it easier to read translations of Chinese poetry than to look at Chinese paintings. They are put off by the absence of color in the ink paintings, and by trying to remember unmanageable names. They feel helpless about ever knowing any artists as individuals, in the way that they know about Leonardo da Vinci, El Greco, or Van Gogh. The decorative arts and the wood-block prints of Japan are more immediately appealing, but the question always comes up: How can you tell Japanese from Chinese art? What makes them different?

You may be standing just outside the Eastern Gate, looking in at an enchanting but unfamiliar world of visual appearances. Not so unfamiliar, our contemporary artists would say. A drawing is a drawing. If you have ever really looked at a Rembrandt drawing, at medieval sculpture, you have something to bring to the arts of China and Japan. If you care about the world of nature, you have something to bring. Bring what you have and explore a little. Then if you do not choose to remain long within the Eastern Gate, you may return, possibly bringing back some new ways of seeing the world around you, some new perceptions about the art and artists of the Western world.

When the great periods of Western art are mentioned—classical, medieval, Renaissance, for instance—most of us can visualize some specific images. We remember a bronze athlete from Greece, a medieval tapestry from France, a Raphael Madonna. But our view of art history in the Far East is blurred. When was T'ang? Where and what was Kamakura?

Members of the younger generation in this country are more likely than the rest of us to have had some contact, in school or college, with the history and arts of the Far East. And travel has made inquirers of thousands of tourists in Japan who have looked up at the Great Buddha of Kamakura, or who have visited the ancient temples of Nara, temples that reflect, in their architecture and their religious images, the T'ang dynasty style, one of the great moments in the arts of China.

Travel in the United States, in Canada, and in Europe can also provide extraordinary opportunities for seeing the paintings, sculpture, and decorative arts of the Far East. Splendid collections are open to the public on the West Coast of the United States, in the Middle West, and in the East. Many of the objects illustrated in the following pages have been chosen from museums that are easily accessible in order to encourage readers to go and look for themselves at original works of art. There is no better way to train the eyes and to develop a personal taste.

This book is intended then, not as condensed art history for beginners (several excellent texts exist), but as something more personal, more informal—an invitation to enter, to look, to study if you will, and to enjoy.

J.G.M.

An Invitation to the Arts of China

1
NATURE AND THE ARTS IN CHINA

Peking, that rectangular city on the North China plain, faces due south. In the Forbidden City at its center, in earlier times, the emperor would sit on his throne with his back to the north, the region of cold winds and troublesome barbarians. Anyone who has lived in Peking must remember vividly having experienced there a strong orientation to the points of the compass. Since the streets run north and south, or east and west, one never loses a clear sense of the four directions. Even in the simple domestic task of hanging a scroll painting, if you are going to place it on the north wall of the living room, you ask to have the nail moved a little to the east or to the west, if you please, instead of saying as we would, a little to the right or to the left. There is something reassuring about this feeling of being set squarely down on the earth under a wide heaven, in a tradition of city planning that goes far back into Chinese history. The old walls that used to surround Peking have disappeared now, in the wake of modernization. The Eastern Gate is a figurative one, through which we may enter a fascinating civilization.

From the parks and lakes of the palace and the leafy courtyards of the city, from colorful fruit and vegetable markets, and from the starlit sky at night, one is always in touch with nature and the changing seasons in Peking. A succession of potted plants for house and courtyard has traditionally marked off the four seasons: the flowering plum for spring, peonies for summer, chrysanthemums for fall, miniature orange and lemon trees in winter. Even within the busy city of Peking in days not long past, people also enjoyed many small and intimate details from the world of nature. Whistles attached to the tails of pigeons made delicate music overhead. Portly businessmen tucked crickets in gourd containers inside their winter coats, so that their bodies' warmth would cause the crickets to chirp, a cheerful accompaniment to a daily stroll.

Another memorable experience of China is a journey up the Yangtze River from the level plains at Hankow (now called Wuhan) to Chungking in Szechuan Province—from the embroidered agricultural landscape of the great river valley through spectacular gorges into a mountainous region, once part of the ancient state of Shu.

Gorges of the Yangtze Photograph by Dmitri Kessel

A Japanese scholar, traveling up the Yangtze to lecture at a university, once arrived in a state of collapse from having identified so many sites famous in history, literature, and art. Those who are steeped in the Western classical tradition might begin to share that kind of experience when cruising among the Greek islands or traveling along the old Roman roads in Italy and Southern France.

For me that very special journey began in a small, four-passenger mail plane that followed the course of the Yangtze River westward. When we came to the gorges, the plane flew so that its wing tips seemed to scrape the sheer vertical walls on either side. To the north and south rose peaks ten thousand feet tall. On this majestic flight, and on the return trip on a small British freighter down the wild rapids, my only reading matter was a small volume of Arthur Waley's translations of Chinese poetry, from which I quote a part of Po Chu-i's "Alarm at First Entering the Yangtze Gorges," written in the year 818:

> Above, a mountain ten thousand feet high:
> Below, a river a thousand fathoms deep.
> A strip of green, walled by cliffs of stone:
> Wide enough for the passage of a single reed.
> At Chü-t'ang a straight cleft yawns:
> At Yen-yu islands block the stream.
> Long before night the walls are black with dusk;
> Without wind white waves rise.
> The big rocks are like a flat sword:
> The little rocks resemble ivory tusks.[1]

Such a journey, especially a flight over the mountains with its shifting perspectives, teaches one an enormous respect for the painters of the tall landscape scrolls, for the way in which trees, rocks, rivers, waterfalls, mists, and mountains are set down, sometimes in subtle washes, sometimes in brilliant shorthand brushstrokes, or in a combination of the two. And during the return journey by riverboat through the gorges and later along the level plain, I realized what distillation of experience, often of travel by water, is also expressed in the long horizontal landscape scrolls.

Suppose for the sake of comparison and contrast we look at two paintings, one by an American nineteenth-century artist, the other by a thirteenth-century Chinese. The title of the American painting, *Kindred Spirits,* is taken from a poem by John Keats; Asher B. Durand (1796–1886) has represented his friends, the painter Thomas Cole and the poet William Cullen Bryant, looking out over a ravine in the Catskills. Painted in oils on canvas, trees, rocks, and foliage are rendered in meticulous detail by the artist's brush. The small fan-shaped painting, *Scholars Conversing Beneath Blossoming Plum,* by Ma Yuan (active c. 1190–c. 1225) is painted in ink and slight color on silk. The two scholars,

Ma Yuan *Scholars Conversing
Beneath Blossoming Plum*

Asher B. Durand *Kindred
Spirits* American

both undoubtedly poets as well, appear more at ease, more comfortably installed in nature, than their American counterparts. Rocks, trees, and distant hills are merely suggested. There is little descriptive detail, only the evocation of an atmosphere. James Cahill observed that the two seated figures, like a pair of parentheses, enclose nothing but express a perfect accord.

This juxtaposition may be a little unfair, since Ma Yuan was one of the old masters of Chinese painting with a long tradition behind him. Asher Durand, on the other hand, lived in a new country, at one remove from the European tradition. He was faced with the problem of how to deal with the wilderness, a new subject for painters. It was, however, a moment when writers and artists shared many of the same ideas, and when nature was approached by Americans with a feeling of awe and reverence.

One of the games we may play to sharpen perceptions about the organization of a picture is to see what happens to a composition when the shape of the external boundaries is changed. If you will trace the fan-shaped outline of Ma Yuan's onto a sheet of typewriter-size paper, cut out the inside, and lay the sheet over "Kindred Spirits," you will be able to change the composition by moving the new frame over the surface of the painting. You can slide the frame around until the over-arching tree begins to show a superficial resemblance to Ma Yuan's tree. You may also notice for the first time how skillfully the Chinese artist has echoed the curve of the fan in the outlines of his seated figures.

To carry this comparison a little further, let us look at another painting, "Schroon Mountain" by Thomas Cole (1801–1848), the founder of the Hudson River School. The time is autumn, with the rich deep tones

Thomas Cole
Schroon Mountain, Adirondacks American

of the forest. It is an impenetrable forest; no pathways invite the viewer to travel in that landscape. The only human beings are a few tiny Indians in a canoe crossing the lake, and the head and shoulders of an Indian appearing as if from nowhere in the underbrush.

Travelers in Autumn Mountains by Sheng Mou (active first half of fourteenth century) presents four tiny figures entering from the lower right-hand corner. We feel that they will be able to continue along a lower road, or to go up and over the shoulder of the mountain. Nature may be grander here than in the Adirondacks, but people make their way along well-traveled paths. We know that Chinese painters were indefatigable travelers, sometimes through the force of circumstances, sometimes traveling in order to visit temples, monasteries, or sites famous in history and literature.

Sheng Mou *Travelers in Autumn Mountains*

Whole books have been produced about the wonderfully varied regions of China (which is almost as large as all of Europe) and about the ways in which Chinese artists at different periods have expressed the character of the landscape they knew. They seldom painted a particular view. Although they sometimes sketched while walking in the mountains, it was not a personal view of a slice of nature that concerned the Chinese, but the *idea* of nature based on many levels of feeling and thinking.

*Austere Mountains and
Ancient Pines* Photograph

*Fantastic Mountains and
Winding Rivers* Photograph

Sloping down toward the sea from the high plateaus of Central Asia, from the mountainous sources of the Yellow River and the Yangtze, China presents a marvelously varied landscape. In the north are austere mountains and ancient pines; in the center, the great fertile river valleys; and south of the Yangtze, lakes and luxuriant vegetation, bamboo forests, fantastic mountains, and winding rivers. Within that varied natural world exists a wealth of trees and plants, of birds and animals, of fish and insects, along with the fabulous beasts of the imagination. And from the beginnings of Chinese art, through all the changes of style and period, the flora, the fauna, and the imaginary creatures, even the rocks, have been represented with a rhythmic vitality, an energy, a spirit, that varies from one age to another, but is almost always recognizably Chinese.

Chimera
Third century

2
THIS WORLD AND THE NEXT
Confucianism, Taoism, and the Rise of Buddhism

This sense of rhythmic vitality moving through all the forces of nature is involved in one way or another with three ways of thought, sometimes called the "three religions" of China. We will try to consider in this chapter some of the ways in which Confucianism and Taoism influenced the visual arts and how the forms of a foreign religion—Buddhism—were, in turn, transformed by the Chinese spirit.

CONFUCIANISM

Confucius, born in the sixth century B.C., in the late Chou period, lived in a small feudal state in what is now the province of Shantung. It was a time of upheaval and social change when many small states were contending for power. A scholar and teacher, Confucius wanted to develop in educated men a feeling of responsibility for the maintenance of tradition and for the orderly processes of government. He believed that cultivated men, trained in ethics and in aesthetics (especially music and poetry), were the best hope for a stable government; that respect for one's elders, for the wisdom of early rulers, for ritual observance, would promote the welfare of humanity. One of the ideals of the Confucian scholar was expressed by the character *jen,* "human-heartedness."

Confucius traveled from state to state, looking for an enlightened ruler willing to listen to his teaching but without much success. The writings which he is thought to have put together became known as the Classics. Along with the *Analects,* a collection of anecdotes about his teaching, the Confucian Classics have been a shaping force in Chinese culture for twenty-five hundred years. If Confucius is now out of favor, banished from the People's Republic of China, it may be because his ideas, or rather his ideas as codified by later generations, are still a force to be reckoned with.

It was not until the Han dynasty (206 B.C.–A.D. 221) that the Confucian Classics assumed a central place in what was by this time a united and powerful empire. The gentlemen scholars of the Confucian tradition began to be concerned not only about the content of literature but about its visual appearance. The writing of Chinese characters, or calligraphy, was looked upon as an art in itself and a personal accomplishment. Since the brush was the tool for both calligraphy and painting, these two arts had much in common. Calligraphy and painting along with poetry and music were thought to be the only arts worthy of gentlemen. Sculpture and the crafts remained the province of artisans. Since both discipline and spontaneity were necessary for the dynamic vitality of each individual Chinese written character, the accomplishment of the Chinese scholar in the art of calligraphy was fundamental to the art of painting.

TAOISM

Tao (pronounced Dow) in Chinese means the way, the road. Sometimes the word is used in a general sense as in the "*tao* of Confucianism," which would be the way of right moral and social action. But Taoism itself is altogether different from the rational and ethical concerns of Confucius. It is the way of intuition, of creativity, of a search for a harmonious relation with the mysterious forces of nature.

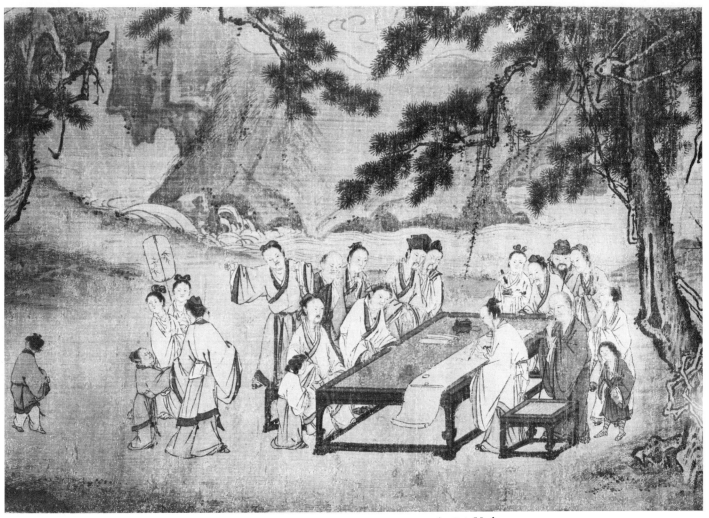

Artist Unknown
Composing Poetry on a Spring Outing

The quotation that follows is from the *Tao te ching,* a poem attributed to Lao Tzu, about whom very little is known. He is thought to have lived in the sixth century B.C., but the poem was probably not compiled until about two hundred years later.

> Thirty spokes share the wheel's hub;
> It is the center hole that makes it useful.
> Shape clay into a vessel;
> It is the space within that makes it useful.
> Cut doors and windows for a room;
> It is the holes which make it useful.
> Therefore profit comes from what is there;
> Usefulness from what is not there.[1]

If the value of a bowl is in the empty space it encloses, then the value of mountains lies in the valleys they enclose. The Tao, like water, seeks the low places. Mountains, valleys, water, and mists became the great

閑來隱几枕書眠又夢入
壺中別有天彷彿玆
身親面目大還真訣得
親傳晋昌唐寅為
東原先生寫圖

T'ang Yin *Dreaming of Immortality in a Thatched Hut*

subject of landscape painting; even the name for landscape in Chinese is *shan-shui*, "mountain-water" picture.

Chuang Tzu, who lived around 300 B.C., left writings that are full of imagination, of paradox, and of a kind of native mysticism. Like the *Tao te ching,* his writings have been a pervasive influence in Taoist thought, and an integral part of Chinese literature. Perhaps the most often quoted passage from his work is about how Chuang Tzu dreamed he was a butterfly. When he woke up, he was unable to decide which he really was: Chuang Tzu who had dreamed he was a butterfly, or a butterfly dreaming he was Chuang Tzu.

During the Han dynasty, this poetic and philosophic Taoism began to develop in other directions. There was a search for immortality through meditation, through diet and control of the breath, and through alchemy. Later a host of new divinities appeared—spirits, ghosts, demons, and immortals—some of them borrowed from the new faith of Buddhism, all eventually incorporated in a kind of folk religion tinged with magic.

For the arts, Taoism was of immense importance. At one level, craftsmen and artisans, close to the materials provided by nature, often discovered their best ways of working through intuition and experience rather than through rational analysis. At the highest level, the great

landscape painters, who were generally Confucian scholars by training and sometimes government officials as well, found their deepest insights in Taoist perceptions of nature and of the nature of creativity.

BUDDHISM

The historical Buddha was born in the sixth century B.C., a prince of the Shakya tribe, probably in the region of India that is now a part of Nepal. Protected by his father's concern from knowledge of disease, old age, and death, Prince Siddhartha was surrounded with every luxury, with jewels and flowers and dancing girls. Nevertheless, having caught a glimpse of human sorrows, he chose to leave his beautiful wife and young son to go in search of the causes of suffering.

After six years of wandering as an ascetic, and of extreme self-mortification, this thoughtful prince sat down to meditate under a fig tree. He resisted the temptations of the Evil One. After three days in a trancelike state, enlightenment came to him at dawn. He became the Buddha, the "Awakened One" or the "Enlightened One." Soon afterward, in his first sermon, he preached that the Middle Way is neither the

Taoist Temple at Hua Shan
Photograph

pursuit of desires and pleasure, nor the pursuit of pain and hardship. He taught that life is suffering, that suffering ends only in death, and that death may mean release from suffering if the endless chain of reincarnation (that is, of birth and death and rebirth) has been broken—release into Nirvana. Nirvana has been variously described as the extinction of all desires, the supreme Reality, the state of perfect blessedness. The virtues preached and exemplified by the Buddha were self-discipline and compassion.

The Buddha thought of himself as a reformer and teacher; he warned his followers against thinking of him as divine. But his magnetism and influence were so great, his message so eagerly received, that by the time of his death at the age of eighty, monks and disciples had already begun to weave about him a complex web of religious symbols and doctrine, with a multiplication of scriptures, of Buddhas and Bodhisattvas, of heavens and heavenly beings.

Wherever the knowledge of Buddhism was carried—over the Himalayas into Central Asia, or by sea to Southeast Asia—certain characteristics of the Buddha image came to be recognized: the heightened shape of the top of the head, the snail-curled hair, the jewel or the tuft of hair in the forehead, the long earlobes (from the weight of the jewels he had worn as a young man), the webbed fingers, and the simple garments of a monk. The Buddha was represented standing in a formal, frontal position, or more often, seated in the position of meditation. It was in the gestures of the expressive hands that the meaning of a specific image could be told, as in the raised hand of reassurance, or the open hand of gift-bestowing.

In painted or carved representations, the Buddha was often accompanied by his early disciples or by Bodhisattvas, saintlike beings who had attained Nirvana but who chose instead to bring relief to suffering humanity. The Bodhisattva Kuan Yin was the Compassionate One, the Bodhisattva Maitreya—or "Buddha-to-be"—a kind of Messiah.

The study of Buddhist images is a long, involved subject. We shall only try to suggest how forms that had been developed in India, foreign in conception and appearance, were adopted and adapted into Chinese culture, especially during the fourth, fifth, and sixth centuries A.D. There were setbacks and persecutions for the Buddhist faith from time to time. But the high point for the arts came in the seventh and eighth centuries during the T'ang dynasty—a period of a sophisticated international style in an empire that tolerated many faiths, at a time when merchants and priests of many nationalities lived in the capital city of Ch'ang-an.

The carving of images and of temples directly into a rock site was an Indian tradition that had been brought across Central Asia to a trading outpost in western China, Tun Huang. The discovery of these "Caves of the Thousand Buddhas" by Sir Aurel Stein is one of the fascinating stories of archaeology in the twentieth century. But the cave temples of Yun-kang and of Lung-men in northwest China are more imposing, more spectacular, and at Lung-men more characteristically Chinese in their rhythms, especially in the treatment of secular subjects. The noble procession of the empress and her attendants, so full of linear movement, comes from one of the most impressive cave chapels at Lung-men, and can now be seen at the Nelson Gallery-Atkins Museum in Kansas City. Originally the emperor and his attendants approached the colossal central figure of the seated Buddha from the opposite side.

Many different paths to salvation were defined within the Buddhist faith as it developed in China, among them Esoteric Buddhism (Shingon

Seated Buddha Indian

Standing Buddha Indian

Sakyamuni Buddha Chinese A.D. 477

Bodhisattva Chinese c. A.D. 530

Buddha Vairocana and Attendants A.D. 672–675

Empress and Her Court as Donors Sixth century

and Tendai in Japan), Pure Land (Jodo in Japan), and Ch'an (Zen in Japan). Esoteric Buddhism envisions the historical Buddha as but one manifestation of the divine force that pervades the whole of creation. Understanding the nature of Vairocana, the cosmic Buddha, was transmitted directly from teacher to pupil, so that salvation was limited to the initiated few. But the elaborate ritual surrounding the cult of Vairocana inspired the construction of awesome images in China and Japan.

The Pure Land sect promised salvation in the Western Paradise to all who repeated in faith the name of Amida (or Amitahba) Buddha. This paradise of pavilions and gardens, filled with light and fragrance, with music and heavenly beings, provided a challenge to painters and sculptors, most of them unknown to us by name. They often worked on great cooperative enterprises.

By contrast, the following terse and independent words are a statement of the Ch'an viewpoint:

> A special transmission outside the scriptures;
> No dependence on words;
> Direct pointing to the soul of man;
> Seeing into one's own nature.

Ch'an in China and Zen in Japan both come from the Sanskrit word *dyana* (meditation). An intense concentration or meditation leading to *satori* (enlightenment) is at the core of Ch'an Buddhism. We shall return to Zen in a later chapter on Japanese art. Here we can only suggest that discipline and spontaneity, wit and humor, a rigorous and often apparently irrational training, underlay what has been described as the world's most irreligious religion.

The painting by Lo P'ing on page 37 expresses the spontaneity and irreverence of a traditional Ch'an character, Han Shan, who is said to have lived in the T'ang dynasty, and of his companion Shih Te. These are the closing lines in Gary Snyder's translation of the poems of Han Shan, a name that means Cold Mountain.

> When men see Han-shan
> They all say he's crazy
> And not much to look at—
> Dressed in rags and hides.
> They don't get what I say
> & I don't talk their language.
> All I can say to those I meet:
> "Try and make it to Cold Mountain."[2]

The pervasive influence of Ch'an ideas in the arts of China, and of Zen, at a later time, in Japan can hardly be overestimated:

Lo P'ing
Han-shan and Shih-te

The school of Ch'an with its sophisticated philosophy of intuition, its intense concentration on individual enlightenment, and its sense of the tao or Buddha-nature immanent in nature had an irresistible appeal for artists, writers, and all those who, for longer or shorter periods, sought the life of contemplation. The T'ang poets often refer to their retreat in Ch'an temples or their conversation with Ch'an masters.[3]

It should be added that some of the great masters of Chinese painting were themselves Ch'an monks, Mu Ch'i, for example. In Japan, two of the greatest, Shubun and Sesshu, were Zen priests.

Japanese temples with their sculptured images that survive in and around Nara, near Kyoto, preserve for us the styles of the Sui and T'ang dynasties of China. They were built during the first great wave of Chinese influence in Japan in the sixth and seventh centuries. Zen Buddhism was the impulse for a second wave of influence from China in the thirteenth and fourteenth centuries. And Zen ideas permeated much that we think of as characteristic of Japanese culture—the tea ceremony, flower arranging, the No theatre, architecture, gardens, and ink painting.

3
CHINESE WRITING
The Image of Thought

Chinese writing, Aldous Huxley once said, is almost the artistic image of thought itself—free, various, and unmonotonous. He compared our simple, geometrical letters and Chinese writing in which flowing brushwork is built up into elaborate forms, each form the symbol of a word, distinct and different.

The word *calligraphy* comes from two Greek words that mean beautiful and writing. We who have grown up in the West may never be able to comprehend the complex beauty of Chinese calligraphy. But once upon a time, while observing the delight of some Chinese children in the practicing of characters (a delight not usually associated with homework), it occurred to me that I might make a beginning along with the six-year-olds. When the old-style writing master came to the house where I was visiting, he brought his materials tied up in a neat blue cloth bundle—a round stone dish for grinding ink, books of characters, and rubbings from stone inscriptions, the paper ruled off in squares of various sizes that schoolchildren use, and an assortment of brushes. Dipping a little water onto the stone, Mr. Tsang took a stick of solidified ink between his thumb and forefinger. Starting in the middle of the dish, he ground in increasingly larger circles. It took about ten minutes to grind enough fresh ink for our purposes.

The teacher was very particular about the pose of the body: right foot a little forward, left foot back, chest up, and brush held perpendicular between the thumb and fingers, just so, and with the flat inside of the wrist kept perpendicular to the table. We were told that the brush must be held so firmly that the teacher could not pull it away from our fingers. He said that we must "feel the strength coming up through the whole body and flowing down the arm and out at the tip of the brush." In a horizontal stroke, for example, the top of the stroke should appear even and flowing, but the lower edge uneven and slightly broken from the impact of one's strength. How the brush tip is to be set down, how lifted off at the end of a stroke, are also to be carefully considered and practiced.

Later, the father of the children with whom I was sharing the lesson made this comment: "Mr. Tsang's writing is excellent," he said, "but it lacks brilliance and originality." No one who has ever seen a Chinese scholar writing a sequence of the beautiful big characters can forget the intense concentration of body and mind that goes into each stroke, or the energy that propels his arm and hand.

Brush, ink, ink stone, and paper are called "The Four Treasures of the House of Literature." A great deal of fascinating information has been written about each of them. Brushes were made of the hair of sheep or wolves, of goats or rabbits, or even of a baby's hair or mouse whiskers. Brush-makers knew where the best rabbits came from and where the best hairs came from (along the backbone of the rabbit). Brushes that consist of a core of stiffer hair surrounded by longer softer hairs coming to a point are set into handles, usually of bamboo. There are two main kinds of brush—soft, pliable, and pointed; or stiffer and more blunt. They come in all sizes, from a few hairs to brushes so big that they require both hands on the handle.

Made of pine soot and glue, ink is formed into rectangular sticks or rounded cakes and embellished with carved or molded designs. The best soot came from the best stands of pine in certain areas (the famous Mount Lu was one of the places), and the best glue was ten years old. Old ink, well ripened, was highly valued.

Ink stones, on which to grind fresh ink, might be made of pottery,

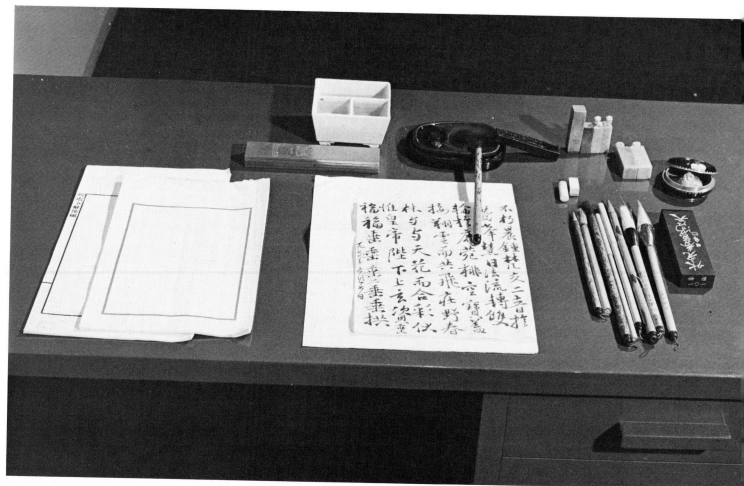

Tools and Materials of the Calligrapher
Photograph by Martin Linsey

but the best were made of a smooth, fine-grained stone found in a special grotto in Kwantung Province. A scholar took great care of his ink stone and saw that it was carefully washed after each use.

The fourth Treasure of the House of Literature, paper, is said to have been invented in A.D. 105. Before that, silk or strips of bamboo were used for writing and painting. Early accounts report that an official named Ts'ai Lun thought of using tree bark, hemp, rags, and fishnets to create sheets of paper. The bark of the mulberry tree along with such materials as rice, straw, and hemp have been used ever since. So the Chinese not only invented paper; they brought papermaking to the highest levels of skill. Knowledge of papermaking was eventually transmitted by Arabs to Spain and did not reach Europe until the twelfth and thirteenth centuries.

Finally, a painter, poet, or calligrapher needed a seal with which to stamp his name, his studio name, or one of his nicknames, in a soft red on the paper. The seal was engraved in archaic characters into ivory, or

An Artist Impressing his Seal
Photograph by the author

jade, or stone. Pressed into a little box or jar of vermilion dye, the seal was then stamped on a painting, usually directly under the artist's written signature. The owner of a painting might add his seal, and so might someone at a later date who admired the painting and wished to add a comment over his own name. The design and cutting of the seal was considered an art in itself, an art in which some of the painters excelled.

For a sense of how the archaic characters still used in the painter's seals relate to the long and varied tradition of brush-written characters, the interested reader is referred to Chiang Yee's *Chinese Calligraphy*. The scholar-calligrapher might write at different times and for different occasions in any of a number of historic styles. His writing could be grave and formal with the *Li-shu* or Official Script and the *K'ai-shu* or Regular Script. He could be lively and temperamental within the freedom of the cursive "running" or "grass" style scripts. It was the "grass" script perhaps that inspired Marianne Moore to write of the East "with its emotional shorthand."

Impression of Seals of the Collector, Liang Ch'ing-piao Photograph

Sun Kung *Seal Characters*

暾將出兮東方　照吾檻兮扶桑　撫余馬兮安驅　夜皎皎兮既明　駕龍輈兮乘雷　載雲旗兮委蛇　長太息兮將上　心低徊兮顧懷　羌聲色兮娛人　觀者憺兮忘歸　緪瑟兮交鼓　簫鍾兮瑤簴　鳴篪兮吹竽　思靈保兮賢姱　翾飛兮翠曾　展詩兮會舞　應律兮合節　靈之來兮蔽日　青雲衣兮白霓裳　舉長矢兮射天狼　操余弧兮反淪降　援北斗兮酌桂漿　撰余轡兮高駞翔　杳冥冥兮以東行　右東君

Ch'u Huan *Li Shu or Official Style*

Kao Shih-ch'i *K'ai Shu or Regular Style*

Chao Meng-fu *Running Style*

Ch'en Shun *Grass Style*

No critical language about any of the arts could possibly be more vivid than the figures of speech used to discuss calligraphy.

Time has not yet vanquished the
    beauty of these letters—
Looking like sharp daggers that pierce
    live crocodiles
Like phoenix mates dancing, like angels hovering down,
Like trees of jade and coral with interlocking branches,
Like golden cord and iron chain tied together tight,
Like incense tripods flung into the sea,
    Like dragons mounting heaven[1]

—HAN YU (768–824)

Su Tung-p'o was a poet, painter, and calligrapher. You will meet him again in the section called "A Literary Interlude." On the twenty-second day of the seventh moon of the year 1077 he wrote down the following words in his own famous handwriting:

Now calligraphy and painting are
the most excellent of all things that
gladden man's heart without
leading him astray.

4
A CHOICE OF ARTISTS
Five Landscape Painters

It seems appropriate to begin the subject of painting by quoting a dialogue between a youth who had been sketching in the mountains and an old man whom he encountered. The setting and the conversation are reported in an essay attributed to Ching Hao, a painter who lived in the tenth century.

Among the T'ai-hang Mountains are deep valleys and large country fields which I used to cultivate when I lived there. One day I climbed the Shen-cheng ridge, which offers a view all around, and on my way back I came to an entrance between two steep cliffs. The moss was dripping with water, strange stones were strewn about, and the

45

mist of good omen was hovering in the air. I entered quickly and found that the place was grown with old pine-trees; the tree in the middle was the largest. The bark of it was overgrown by green lichen and covered by scales. It rose to the sky like a coiling dragon, trying to reach the clouds and dominated the whole forest. The spirit of it was vigorous and its beauty was rich. The smaller trees stood humbly bending down; the roots of some were reaching out of the ground, others were coiling across the water current, others again were suspended on cliffs hanging over the brooks which wound among the moss and the crumbling stones. The sight seemed to me most marvellous; I looked around with deepest admiration.

The following day I returned to the same place bringing my brushes along and made some pictures of the trees trying to render their real nature. Then in the spring of the following year, as I was walking among the Stone Drum Cliffs, I met an old man who asked me what I had been doing. When I told him about it, he said to me: "Do you know the method of painting?" To which I answered: "You seem to be an old uncouth rustic; how could you know anything about brush-work?" But the old man said: "How can you know what I carry in my bosom?" Then I listened and felt ashamed and astonished, as he spoke to me as follows: "Young people like to study in order to accomplish something; they should know that there are six essentials in painting. The first is called spirit, the second is called harmony (or, resonance), the third is called thoughts (plans), the fourth is called motif (scenery), the fifth is the brush, and the sixth is the ink." I remarked: "Painting is to make beautiful things, and the important point is to obtain their true likeness; is it not?" He answered: "It is not. Painting is to paint, to estimate the shapes of things and really obtain them, to estimate the beauty of things and reach it, to estimate the reality (significance) of things and grasp it. One should not take outward beauty for reality; he who does not understand this mystery, will not obtain the truth, even though his pictures may contain likeness." I asked: "What is likeness and what is truth?" The old man said: "Likeness can be obtained by shapes without spirit; but when truth is reached, spirit and substance are both fully expressed. He who tries to express spirit through ornamental beauty will make dead things." I thanked him and said: "From this I realize that the study of calligraphy and painting is an occupation for virtuous men; I am only a farmer and have not understood it; I have been playing with the brush, but not accomplished anything; I feel quite ashamed to receive your kind explanations of the essentials in art which were unknown to me."[1]

The six essentials of painting, about which the old man spoke, had already been set down by Hsieh Ho in slightly different form at the end of the fifth century. Spirit, and harmony or resonance (sometimes translated as cosmic energy or rhythmic vitality), have always been the primary concern of the Chinese painter. It came to be believed that this "spirit resonance" must be born in a painter; it could not be acquired by study, although disciplined study of the old masters was essential in order to understand the traditions of the past and to be able to add something new of one's own.

Except for murals on the walls of palaces and temples, paintings were made on silk or on paper. Differences in quality of the material and of sizing provided a variety of possible surfaces.

There are three main forms for painting, the vertical or hanging scroll, the horizontal or hand scroll, and the album leaf. In general, the hanging scrolls are taller and narrower than our familiar painting shapes, and the hand scrolls are longer, sometimes much longer, than our horizontal paintings. Album leaves may be round or slightly oval, taking their shape from fans; or they may be rectangular. They are usually mounted and kept in boxes or portfolios, much as we handle unframed prints and drawings.

Watercolors are made of minerals or of vegetable dyes. Ink is made of pine soot and glue, sometimes with the addition of other elements. The quality of the ink may be cool, tending toward bluish-black, or warm, tending toward brownish-black. Ink may be glossy or mat. One of the chief resources of the monochrome-ink painter is the whole range of tones from the richest black through delicate grays to the whiteness of paper or silk. How ink can be used to suggest color is an intriguing subject that was of great interest to Chinese artists. The Chinese writer, Chiang Yee, observed that only those of us who take our coffee black will be able to appreciate the ink paintings. Sugar and milk, he says, like color, are a superficial distraction.

Unfamiliar to us is the habit of inscribing paintings with poems or comments, sometimes written directly on the paintings or mounted at the extreme left-hand end of the hand scrolls. Nothing in Western art is comparable to the close bond between poetry and painting that existed in China. Poetry as an integral part of "literary men's painting" is founded on the idea that ink painting is an art of the Confucian gentleman and scholar—one who is learned in classical texts, able to compose verse for any occasion, and to write it down in his own accomplished and personal handwriting. In Hugh Honour's phrase, the poems that are inscribed on Chinese paintings are "like human voices in orchestral music."[2] Comments that follow a painting may provide a history of the collectors and connoisseurs who have owned, or seen and appreciated, the work. Called colophons, these comments provide dates, anecdotes, and a variety of critical and biographical information, often covering hundreds of years.

Handwritten signatures, inscriptions on the paintings, and colophons are usually concluded with a stamped seal in red. Self-important collectors, including the Ch'ien Lung emperor in the eighteenth century, stamped their names prominently and often, to the dismay of true connoisseurs.

In the Egyptian galleries at the Cleveland Museum, a little girl, with great seriousness, once asked this question: "Do the Egyptians come before or after the dinosaurs?" "After the dinosaurs," she was told, "and before Christ." Her question illustrates the problem we all have in fitting together the events of times past. The following notes may help to place five Chinese artists in your mental filing case of European art.

Li Ch'eng (919–967) lived in the tenth century, a time from which no single name of a European artist is familiar to the general public today. Landscape painting as such had not existed since Roman times. The great murals and illuminated books of the Romanesque style were still to come, and they were often by artists unknown to us by name.

When Ma Yuan lived (1190–1225) during the Southern Sung dynasty in China, the style known as High Gothic prevailed in medieval France. Some of the artists, sculptors, and designers of Europe are known by name to art historians, but there are no memorable names known to us all. The building of the nave of Chartres Cathedral (1194–1220), a great corporate enterprise, almost exactly corresponds to the dates of Ma Yuan's life.

Chao Meng-fu (1254–1322), who brought a new direction to Chinese painting, was a contemporary of Giotto (1276?–?1337). Giotto also brought a new direction to art in Italy, and eventually to the art of Western Europe. A link with Italy in Chao Meng-fu's lifetime was the appearance of Marco Polo in "Cathay," in the cities of Peking and Hangchou and many others. Marco Polo might possibly have encountered the painter and statesman, Chao Meng-fu, at the court of Kublai Khan. But as a merchant of Venice in the service of the Mongol emperor, Marco Polo would probably never have seen, or been able to understand, the aristocratic and personal art of Chao Meng-fu.

In the last two decades of Shen Chou's life (1427–1509), the period of his most characteristic work, Leonardo da Vinci was painting *The Last Supper,* and Columbus, looking for a passage to the Orient, was discovering America.

And lastly, when the Chinese painter Tao-Chi (1641–c. 1710) was born in one of the southernmost provinces of China, Rubens (1577–1640) had just died in Flanders. In Holland, Rembrandt (1606–1669) was about to paint his first masterpiece, *The Night Watch* (1642). Tao-Chi lived into the first years of the eighteenth century, a period that was to bring to China new contacts with European artists and with merchants from Europe and from America.

Here, then, from the long story of Chinese painting, are brief accounts of five landscape painters.

LI CH'ENG *(919–967)*

Landscapes are large objects and he who looks at them must do so from a distance if he is to grasp the form, the position, the spirit, and the image of mountains and streams.[3]

In relation to the arts of all the great world cultures, Chinese landscape painting stands as one of the supreme achievements. During the T'ang dynasty (618–907), that time of world empire when the Chinese were immensely proud of their achievements, and when Buddhism was at its height, figure painting was a more important subject for artists than landscape. But nearly a thousand years before European painters saw the landscape for itself, and not just as a background for figures, Chinese artists were evolving a whole pictorial language to express the majesty of mountains, the movement of clouds and mists, the rhythm of water, the wonder of ancient trees, and the varied forms of rocks and cliffs. Through brush and ink, the great artists of the tenth and eleventh centuries were able to express their sense of the unity of all nature, animate and inanimate, suffused with that quality of "spirit harmony" or "spirit resonance," that "breath" they called *ch'i yun.*

Wang Wei, who lived in the eighth century, is credited with being the father of monochrome ink painting in contrast to decorative and finely detailed landscapes in color known as the "blue and green" style. Although his poetry survives, no paintings can surely be assigned to Wang Wei.

In the style of the eighth century, although probably later in actual date, is a well-known work in the Palace Museum in Taipei, *The Emperor Ming Huang's Journey to Shu,* painted in ink and color on silk. The court

Artist Unknown
The Emperor Ming Huang's Journey to Shu

ladies and gentlemen traveling through the mountains present a picture of great decorative charm, but in marked contrast to the unity and power of the ink painting, *Buddhist Temple Amid Clearing Mountain Peaks,* that we will now consider. Attributed to Li Ch'eng (pronounced Lee Chung), this painting is probably by a somewhat later hand, but preserving the special qualities of his style.

Of Li Ch'eng we know that he was born in 919, that his father and grandfather were distinguished scholars and administrators, that he painted for his own satisfaction and not in order to make a living, and that he died in 967.[4] He lived in the period following the T'ang, known as the Five Dynasties, and into the first years of the Northern Sung. It is the grandeur of the northern landscape that he painted, and his style is associated with the austerity of autumn and winter scenes.

In the painting *Buddhist Temple Amid Clearing Mountain Peaks,* we see rocky banks of a stream, a little bridge, an inn for pilgrims, gnarled trees with "crab-claw" branch tips that surround a temple complex with its hexagonal tower on the height. Slightly separated by mists behind the temple rises the dominant mountain, with passages into more distant space on either side. The eye is led upward in diagonal steps from the base of the picture to the summits of the mountains.

The miracle of this painting is the convincing organic structure of the whole. A broken twisting brush line indicates the outer forms of mountain masses, but the internal structure is built of many paler ink brushstrokes, sometimes long slender strokes, sometimes almost triangular spots set down by the brush tip. These brushstrokes or *"t'sun"* were later classified into a whole vocabulary to be drawn on by generations of artists: the "rain-drop *t'sun,*" the "hemp fibre *t'sun,*" the "ax-cut *t'sun,*" and many others.

By his contemporaries and followers, Li Ch'eng was thought to share in the creative powers of Nature itself. Because he does not allow his own mannerisms, his own emotions, to come between us and the experience of nature, we may say that this is a painting of great power and yet of classical restraint. With three or four other works by artists slightly younger, and acknowledging their debt to Li Ch'eng, we encounter in the tenth and eleventh centuries paintings which the Chinese feel have never been surpassed and that are designated by traditional criticism as belonging to a class of paintings regarded as "divine."

MA YUAN *(active from about 1190–1225)*

Ma Yuan lived about two hundred and fifty years after Li Ch'eng. The scene had shifted from the imposing mountain landscape of the north, and a political capital at Kaifeng on the Yellow River, to the gentler landscape around the city we know as Hangchou, southwest of Shanghai.

Attributed to Li Ch'eng
*Buddhist Temple Amid
Clearing Mountain Peaks*
(see also pages 52 and 66)

The Tartars had captured Kaifeng in 1127 and carried away the emperor, Hui Tsung, to exile and to death. The Imperial Academy of Painting, which this artist emperor founded, and his great collection of paintings were dispersed.

A young prince who escaped capture finally managed to establish himself and his court at Hangchou in the region known as Chiangnan, "south of the river," that is, south of the Yangtze. In an uneasy peace bought by paying enormous tribute to the Tartars, the remnants of the Sung Empire were gathered about a luxury-loving and nostalgic court. Marco Polo, writing at the end of the thirteenth century, called Hangchou the most beautiful city in the world, although he himself came from Venice with its canals and lagoons and lacelike palaces, its prosperous merchants and busy craftsmen. Hangchou is still famous for gardens and villas, for the beauty of the West Lake, for the pavilions in the lake, the fragrance of lotus, for tea plantations and temples on the surrounding hills. All of this remains a dream in the mind of anyone who has ever had the good fortune to visit Hangchou.

It was in this setting that painters like Ma Yuan of the re-established Imperial Academy lived and worked. Of the fourth generation of a family of professional artists, Ma Yuan was followed by a talented son, Ma Lin.

We have already discussed briefly a fan-shaped album leaf by Ma Yuan, *Scholars Conversing Beneath Blossoming Plum.* If you will turn back to page 22, you will see that in comparison to Li Ch'eng's noble

Attributed to Li Ch'eng *Buddhist Temple Amid Clearing Mountain Peaks* (detail)
(see also pages 50 and 66)

prospect, Ma Yuan has chosen a much more limited outlook. There is no spectacular mountain view. It is almost as if the vibrant space enclosed by the two scholars were the subject of the painting.

In an album leaf in the Palace Museum in Taipei, a scholar under a willow tree seems to be looking up at a pair of orioles while a young boy carries his musical instrument, the *ch'in.* The weight of the composition is all at the lower left (it is easy to see why the artist was called "One-corner Ma"), but the poetic mood is held in balance by the evocation of space that occupies the upper right. The poem in translation reads like this:

> "Brushed by his sleeves, wild flowers dance in the wind;
> fleeing from him, the hidden birds cut short their songs."[5]

In a hand scroll in the Cincinnati Art Museum, *Four Sages of Shang Shan,* the artist employs again those marvelously graded ink washes to suggest atmosphere and space, but his foreground brushstrokes, strong and angular or sparkling in their variety, play the more important part. The subject of the painting was well known. In a time of trouble, about 200 B.C., four wise old men withdrew into the mountains, a recurring theme in Chinese painting and poetry. One of the forty colophons which follows the painting makes this comment:

> It is better to be poor than to sing perpetually of riches and honors.
> They retired into obscurity and lived on mushrooms
> To escape from the harsh rule of the Ch'in.
> Shang-shan being gone these thousand years,
> Who is there to continue the noble tradition of these men?[6]

Let us try to examine the scroll on the next page as if we were able to hold it in our hands and to unroll it slowly from its beginning at the extreme right. Our eyes will compose and recompose the painting continuously as we unroll and reroll the whole nine-foot length. Museums usually have to show hand scrolls opened out from one end to the other in glass cases. Reproductions in books often divide a scroll into sections. But in handling the scroll itself on a table, you would look at no more of the painting at one time than you could conveniently hold between your two hands. And if you were a Chinese collector of paintings, you might share your enjoyment with two or three congenial companions.

The painting opens with a motif of cresting waves against moving water. Then come sharply cut rocks, boldly stated, followed by dizzying whirls of pine needles above the heads of the four recluses. One of the sages is presumably looking for mushrooms. He is followed by a young boy. Two are playing *go,* a game not unlike chess, while the fourth is an interested observer. The sharp angles of their robes, although indicated in fine brushstrokes, are set down with immense style and conviction. The

肥遯高顏物外遊出山
葛巾自顧庭司匏機識
空字古不携名蹟鞍到
元中題者設十八年
皓賴以蹟身其籍四
吉廬力孚能出枝投右
因題是詩爲之拈出
徽詔詠古者似之既呈
之不藏自是高帝志
兩景定無穆四元筍
調護力也不妹雷楚溪
相持持水大公高請今
一杯芙果今李竹蘭
愛其麼盈而立此喜僑
所頤惜宣俗侯諫料
帝元康靈代義自
右祖之楊非將送料
楚梵群宮童秘事
安跡而傳之遂史多
喜音術下化伯侯予
尤名爲然則此人者
渾紀下老人朱兔稱
石者流師詩題作石
梁雹題友成書漬入續
函踏福福二楊今作老
鐵雹梅載五言束奇得
時劍古情無運覽真弘
誦定甲戌春筆筆

遊跡高橫
一阿陽爪
石友窗中
尤名李松黃
喜音爾宗
有閒春日
祺長訪
依款作
供題

scroll concludes in a fortissimo climax of slashing rocks against a brilliant tangle of tree patterns.

The kind of brushstroke (or *ts'un*) that defines the sloping planes of the rock is known as "big ax-cut," and can be seen most clearly in the final section. The pine needles are said to be of the "cart-wheel" type. "Nail-head" and "rat-tail" *ts'un* have been used in the angled folds of the garments.[7] These conventions of the brushstroke, and others at the disposal of a well-trained artist, might be compared to the differing sounds of musical instruments, on which a composer can draw to build up any desired effect from the orchestra.

Ma Yuan and his contemporary, Hsia Kuei, were much admired by the emperors of the Southern Sung and by the court. Their influence on later painting, however, was stronger in Japan than in China. It is interesting, too, that Chinese painting was introduced to museums and collectors here by scholars trained in the Japanese taste. That is why the names of Ma Yuan and Hsia Kuei are probably still the best known of all Chinese artists in this country.

Outside the circle of the professional artists to which Ma Yuan belonged, there had existed a group of scholars or "literary men" who painted as they practiced calligraphy—for their own pleasure and as a means of self-development and self-expression. The most distinguished and the most engaging of them all was Su Tung-p'o (1037–1101), also known as Su Shih. He lived during the Northern Sung period, but his influence was still strong in Hangchou, where for a while he was governor. A poet of great distinction, a painter of bamboos, and a high government official, Su Tung-p'o had to face the exile and frustrations of public life. Painting as an expression of the character of the man through his brushwork was what mattered to such a scholar, and not painting as the description of a place, or as the projection of a mood. "Anyone who talks about painting in terms of likeness," Su Tung-p'o once wrote, "deserves to be classed with children."

Another group of painters who would have agreed with this statement of Su Tung-p'o were the Ch'an Buddhist monks, living and painting in the monasteries on the hills around Hangchou. We will return to their apparently careless and spontaneous paintings in a discussion of Ch'an, or Zen, in Japan.

Because the work of Li Ch'eng set standards for the art of landscape painting and because of a certain monumental character, we have said that *Buddhist Temple Amid Clearing Mountain Peaks* has a "classic" quality. Because of the emotional involvement of the artist, the expression of a lyrical and poetic mood, we may speak of Ma Yuan's paintings as "romantic." With our next painter, Chao Meng-fu we come to a shift of direction in the art of landscape painting.

Ma Yuan *The Four Sages of Shang Shan*

CHAO MENG-FU *(1254–1322)*

Soon after Ma Yuan died (c. 1225), the northern city we know as Peking was captured by the hard-riding armies of the Mongol conqueror, Genghis Khan. And in another fifty years, the whole prosperous region of the lower Yangtze valley, including the pleasure-loving southern capital of Hangchou, fell to the Mongols. Barbarians from the north and west had been harassing the Chinese for centuries, sometimes driven back, sometimes more or less assimilated into Chinese culture. But never before had they controlled the whole of China. They were the masters of central Asia as well, and at one time their power reached as far as the Danube River.

Most of the scholar-artists, trained in the Confucian tradition, withdrew into retirement, refusing to take service under the Mongol conquerors—to become "collaborators." Chao Meng-fu, from Wu-hsing in the south, was a descendant of one branch of the Sung imperial family. He was presented to Kublai Khan in 1286 and was invited to serve at his court, where he quickly rose to the highest office, becoming first minister and serving under several emperors. He was honored as a scholar; he was governor of two important provinces. He was of such upright character and distinguished appearance, so renowned as calligrapher and painter, that he came to be respected even by those who disapproved of his service under the Mongols. His personal handwriting served as model for the printing types used in the Mongol or Yuan dynasty (as it came to be known).

The softness and poetry of Southern Sung academic painting, as we have seen it in the art of Ma Yuan, was considered by the scholar painters of the Yuan as a sign of the moral weakness that allowed China to fall to the Mongols. And these scholars did not in any way wish to appear to be painting to please the taste of their uncouth conquerors. Two ideas were of special concern. In order to renew a sense of identity with their historic past, the scholar-artists went back beyond the more sentimental Southern Sung to such painters as Tung Yuan and Li Ch'eng, thus giving their work "the air of antiquity." They also wished to emphasize the brushwork itself—"the writing of an idea."

Turning now to the reproduction of *Bamboos, Rocks and Lonely Orchids,* notice the brushstroke that defines the form of the rock. Called "flying white," the hairs of the brush are slightly separated to let the white paper show through the irregular stroke. You will see also that the crisp black leaves—and this is especially clear in the detail—immediately suggest Chinese written characters.

Chao Meng-fu
*Bamboos, Rocks and
Lonely Orchids* (detail)

Chao Meng-fu once wrote:

A rock should look like the "flying white,"
    and a tree like the "seal" stroke;
In writing the bamboo leaves,
    one should first learn the *"pa-fen"* method.
If a person understands this thoroughly,
He will discover that calligraphy and
    painting have always been the same.[8]

In the Freer Gallery in Washington, a short hand scroll, once in the Imperial collection, is called *Sheep and Goat.* There is no foreground, no distant landscape, but the two animals appear to have their feet firmly planted on the ground. The contrast in structure, texture of their coats, and personality, is vividly expressed as can be seen in the illustration on page 58 and the detail on page 67.

Anyone who has ever drawn or painted with an ink-filled brush must look with awe at the goat's hair, parted down that flexible backbone, and at the thick woolly coat of the sheep, his rounded outer edges slightly scalloped to indicate texture, especially noticeable in the dark patches.

Once on a summer day I saw a herd of Holstein cows, black and white, on a steep hillside against a blue sky. White clouds seemed to

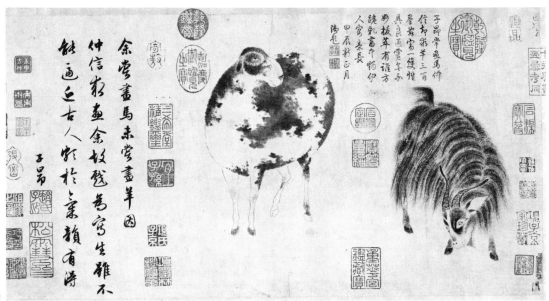

Chao Meng-fu
Sheep and Goat
(see also page 67)

repeat the black-and-white markings of the grazing animals. A phrase remembered from a poem of Gerard Manley Hopkins instantly explained itself to me—"skies of couple-colour as a brinded cow." Perhaps it is fantasy on the part of this writer to see Chao Meng-fu's couple-colored sheep as having a cloudlike appearance—Chinese clouds, of course. Anyway, it is essentially the proud, patient, sheeplike look that lives before us in the painting along with the lively, unpredictable goatishness of the goat.

There is apparently something more in this painting which we could never guess from a casual glance—a symbolic reference to a Chinese general in the year 100 B.C. who was forced by barbarians to tend sheep in the rough country of northwestern China, and of his mournful encounter with a former friend who had deserted to the enemy. At least, this is one meaning of the painting as it was understood by writers of colophons in later years.

But the artist's own inscription at the left written in his famous handwriting is simple and direct:

I have painted horses but have never tried sheep [or goats]. Since Chung-hsin asked me for a painting, I have playfully painted these from life. Although the painting cannot approach those of ancient masters, it seems to have somewhat captured their spirit consonance.

—Tsu-ang (CHAO MENG-FU)[9]

Chao Meng-fu was best known in his own time for paintings of horses mostly set down in color, but since there is much debate over which of his horse paintings may be considered genuine, we have chosen to represent that side of his art by a beautiful example from the work of a follower, Jen Jen-fa. If you look carefully on pages 66 and 67, you may find a surprising and delightful resemblance between each groom and the horse he is leading.

The rule of the Mongols in China, made vivid to us in the West by the writings of Marco Polo, lasted less than a hundred years. Chao

Meng-fu was the greatest master of calligraphy and painting in the first half of that period, and a strong influence on important artists of the next half century. The "Four Great Masters" of the later Yuan are names you will encounter in any book on Chinese painting, Huang Kung-wang, Ni Tsan, Wu Chen, and Wang Meng. They continued the revolution in ink painting begun by Chao Meng-fu, that shift in emphasis from landscape as a subject for painting to brushwork, to the "written" landscape, as of equal if not of more importance than the motif. Along with Chao Meng-fu, the "four masters" were greatly admired by Shen Chou in the fifteenth century and Tao-Chi in the seventeenth, two artists we shall consider next.

SHEN CHOU *(1427–1510)*

Shen Chou provides something of an autobiography in the verses inscribed on his paintings, verses that are always harmonious with the subject and feeling of the painting. He lived in the Ming dynasty, in a more peaceful time than the three painters already considered. Growing up in a comfortable household of scholars and painters on estates that had belonged to his great-grandfather, he lived not far from Suchou. Like Hangchou it is a city famous for its gardens and waterways.

Trained for government service, Shen Chou was able to avoid administrative positions under the plea that it was his duty to look after his widowed mother. He devoted himself to literary study, to painting, to poetry, to hospitality, to the enjoyment of life in the country, and to the intellectual pleasures of the city of Suchou. Shen Chou's mother lived to be a hundred years old, and he came to be greatly admired for his "filial piety," one of the chief Confucian virtues.

Shen Chou's grandfather, father, and uncle were cultivated amateur painters; he learned first from his father and uncle and then from distinguished teachers—artists who were their friends. A very large and famous painting in the Palace Museum in Taipei, *Lofty Mount Lu,* was a birthday gift to one of his teachers. For the "Four Great Masters" of the Yuan dynasty, Shen Chou developed a special admiration. He made a number of paintings in the spare silvery manner of Ni Tsan, and others in the moist ink and terse brushstrokes of Wu Chen.

Although Shen Chou painted many variations on the theme of older masters, he made his own poetic statements that seem more objective, more related to a particular landscape than the romantic evocations of Ma Yuan, less anxious and introspective than the work of Chao Meng-fu and the Four Great Masters of Yuan.

Shen Chou painted a hand scroll, *Return from Stone Lake (Style of Ni Tsan)* in 1466 while journeying homeward on his boat to which he gave the charming name of "Duck-weed Balcony."[10] (The hand scroll is now in the Art Institute of Chicago.) Four hundred years later, on the other side of the world, Daubigny and Claude Monet were painting landscapes from their studio boats along the Seine and the Oise Rivers. One might observe that the tools and equipment needed by a Chinese artist were lighter and more portable than the oil colors and canvas used by traveling artists in nineteenth-century France.

Surely one of the most beautiful, most appealing of works by Shen Chou in this country is the group of album leaves mounted as a hand scroll in the Nelson Gallery-Atkins Museum in Kansas City. Five paintings by Shen Chou make up this scroll with a final album leaf by his brilliant follower and friend, Wen Cheng-ming. Together the two artists were considered the founders of the Wu School of Painting, named for the region around Suchou, and the most influential school of the Ming dynasty.

Shen Chou's album leaf *Three Gardeners in A Fenced Enclosure,* which has already been reproduced as the frontispiece of this book, is the first painting in the group of five. Next comes *Poet on A Mountain,* which stands at the beginning of the chapter on China in "A Literary Interlude." The poem inscribed in four lines at the upper left counterbalances the crisp detail of trees at the lower right.

> White clouds like a belt
>   encircle the mountain's waist
> A stone ledge flying in space
>   and the far thin road.
> I lean on my bramble staff
>   and gazing into space
> Make the note of my flute
>   an answer to the sounding torrent.[11]

The painting is full of air and movement; a light, apparently effortless hand held the brush that indicates the distant mountains and the encircling clouds. But the structure of the promontory that rises like the prow of a ship is boldly stated. Notice, too, the clarity of the ink tones, from the rich black accents through clearly shaded steps to the palest tones and to white. The third painting in this series of album leaves mounted as a hand scroll is called *Man, Bird, and a Boy in a Boat.* It is possible that the boat represents the artist's "Duck-weed Balcony," or it may be that there are symbolic overtones in this picture of a painter with his crane—a symbol of immortality. In any case the handling of ink is more crisp, the leaves and pine needles more strictly patterned than in *Three Gardeners in A Fenced Enclosure* or *Poet on A Mountain.*

Apparently poems now lost were once attached to the album leaves in the Cleveland Museum of Art. The eight paintings all represent scenes in and around Tiger Hill in Suchou. The composition of *The Sword Spring* that seems to extend beyond the edges of the paper presents interesting

Shen Chou *Man, Bird, and Boy in a Boat*

Shen Chou *The Sword Spring*

space relations. The three men standing on a flat rock are enclosed by projecting cliffs on either side—cliffs that form what is sometimes called a "space cell." A second "cell" seems to be indicated to the right, while beyond the pavilion still deeper space is indicated. There is, however, a certain ambiguity about what is near and what is far that gives an ambivalence, a quality of movement, to the whole surface. Remembering that such a painting was set down directly (no corrections or reworking are possible with brush and ink), one must marvel at the sureness of placement, the rhythmic order of brushstrokes, the clarity of tone in the washes, and the sparkle of ink dots that enliven the whole. Such a combination of subtlety and conviction is surely the mark of a master hand.

TAO-CHI *(1641–c.1717)*

> Mountains and rivers compel me to speak for them: the mountains and rivers are transformed through me, and I am transformed through them. Therefore I design my paintings around all the extraordinary peaks which I have sought out.
>
> —Tao-Chi[12]

Born in one of the southernmost provinces of China, from childhood Tao-Chi had known mountains and the beautiful remote sites of Buddhist temples and monasteries. In the troubled times at the fall of the Ming dynasty, the Manchus were gaining control of China. Tao-Chi's father, who was descended from one line of the Ming imperial family, lost his life in an effort to gain the throne. It is said that Tao-Chi, at the age of four, was entrusted to a family servant to make his escape, and that he eventually entered a Buddhist monastery for protection. He adopted the Buddhist name of Tao-Chi; he was also known as Shih T'ao (stone wave) and by other names at different times, including "Friar Bitter Melon."

With an older brother monk, Tao-Chi apparently spent the next twenty years or so wandering in the Yangtze River area where Buddhist retreats could be found at the famous mountain and lake sites of that fabulous region. In Anhwei Province he came to know important painters and poets, some of the most original talents of his time. Under the Manchu rule, Confucian scholars, painters, and poets shared an uneasy political situation, so that wherever they traveled they were drawn together in gatherings that must have been stimulating to Tao-Chi in the development of his own special gifts. One painting of his, now in the museum in Suchou, *Ten Thousand Ugly Ink Blots,* seems to concentrate within itself the protests and frustrations of a talented artist. James Cahill called this group of artists the "Fantastics and Eccentrics." Tao-Chi was the most original, the most creative of them all.

After the wandering years, Tao-Chi settled down in his own "One-Branch Studio" at a well-known Buddhist temple outside of Nanking. There one day in 1684 he was presented to the Manchu emperor, K'ang Hsi. For the last years of his life, except for an interval of three

Tao-Chi
Ten Thousand Ugly Ink Blots (detail)

years in Peking, Tao-Chi lived in the great commercial and cultural city of Yangchou on the Grand Canal. There, in a country at peace under the ablest of the Manchu emperors, K'ang Hsi, Tao-Chi gave up his Buddhist connections and lived more or less as a professional artist. He is reported to have designed gardens in Yangchou using those famous tall rocks with pierced openings that were, for the Chinese, what we today might call "found sculpture." They were an integral part of garden design.

Tao-Chi knew and admired the old masters of Chinese painting whose work he had special opportunity to see in great private collections in Peking. But he was impatient of less perceptive, less gifted artists who were content to copy the manner of the old masters without communicating anything of their spirit. "The method," he wrote, "which consists in not following any method is the perfect method."[13] So Tao-Chi came to be looked upon as an "individualist," as a "rebel," in contrast to the more conventional painters of the Ch'ing dynasty, especially those known as the "Four Wangs," who were officially favored and collected.

A special appeal of Tao-Chi's work for us today lies in his ability to convey the wonders and delights of nature, whether in the great mountain landscapes, in a still life of root vegetables, or in a single branch of flowering plum. For the means by which he expressed that special joy, that sense of elation, we can only try to give a few clues in examining reproductions of three or four paintings. Fortunately, there are fine examples of Tao-Chi's work in both public and private collections in this country.

In *Peach-blossom Spring* (on pages 120 and 121, in " A Literary Interlude"), rich tones of deep blue and green predominate with contrasting accents of soft rose-red. The subject of the painting has been interpreted over and over again by Chinese artists, the story of a fisherman who chanced upon a passageway through the mountains that led to a lost land where people still lived in a dreamlike golden age. You will find the story as told by T'ao Ch'ien (A.D. 365–427) on page 119, in "A Literary Interlude." In the painting, you will see the fisherman's abandoned boat at the head of the stream he had been following.

Emerging from the mountain, still holding his oar, the fisherman is met by three inhabitants of the hamlet. On a distant misty field, a farmer is plowing; the ink that indicates his little bull has been allowed to run with easy abandon.

Spring on the Min River also employs color, this time for delicate atmospheric effect in tones of softest beige and pink-apricot. The artist has inscribed a fairly long poem in his own vigorous and personal hand. It begins like this:

> Under the Yangtzu Bridge, where the river overflows,
> The willow tendrils show forth their hue insensitive to man's grey
>   hair.
> Throughout Spring, rain and snow have kept away the scenery lovers;
> Yet throughout Ch'ing-ming season, the plum blossoms will preserve
>   and flourish.
> Aging and being useless, I have grown attached to my friends;
> But year after year, my friends have scattered like stars and seagulls.[14]

Tao-Chi *Spring on the Min River*

Tao-Chi *Spring on the Min River* (detail)

For what is painting [he wrote] but the great method of changes and developments in the universe? The spirit and essence of hills and streams, the development and growth of the creation, the action of the forces of the *yin* and the *yang*, all are revealed by the brush and ink for the depiction of this universe and for our enjoyment.[15]

Tao-Chi *Study in Wet Ink (Waterside Hut)*

Turning now from hand scrolls to album leaves, it seems clear that the intimate size of the page, and the sequential grouping of subjects must have had a special interest for Tao-Chi. Just as distinguished as the larger scroll paintings are the small album leaves in public and private collections in this country, in England, and in the Far East. They provide an extraordinary variety of subject, of handling, and of mood. In the painting called *Study in Wet Ink (Waterside Hut),* shown above, we look over a great rock, suffused with light, past treetops and water to two small houses on a rocky promontory and the distant hills beyond. The time seems to be evening or possibly moonlight.

In painting, Tao-Chi felt that one stroke led to another until the whole was held in dynamic balance, a creative act on the part of the artist parallel to the creative forces of nature and of life itself.

Attributed to Li Ch'eng
*Buddhist Temple Amid
Clearing Mountain Peaks*
(see also pages 50 and 52)

Chao Meng-fu *Sheep and Goat* (detail)
(see also page 58)

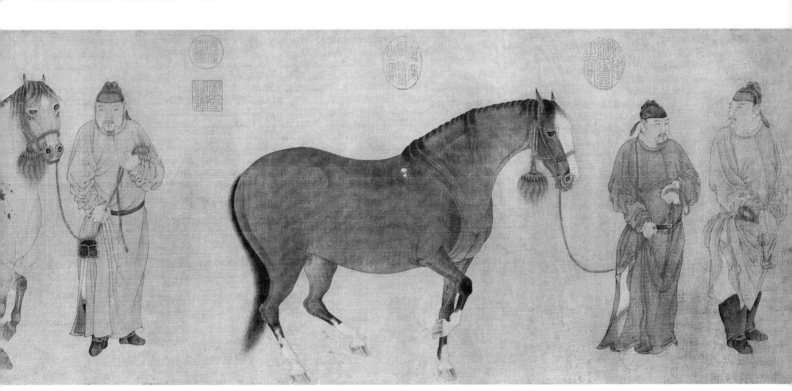

Jen Jen-fa *Three Horses and Four Grooms*

5
THE CERAMIC TRADITION

Only by the form, the pattern,
Can words or music reach
The stillness, as a Chinese jar still
Moves perpetually in its stillness.

—*T. S. Eliot*[1]

If you have ever dug your fingers into wet clay, rolled coils, and shaped them into a bowl; if you have ever watched a potter at a revolving wheel, shaping a lump of clay into a tall vessel—into what seems a living form—you have encountered the fundamentals of the ceramic tradition. And if you have been privileged to glance through the quickly opened door of a kiln at the incandescent pots, all glowing red and orange, you have some sense of the magical transformations that take place during the firing of a kiln.

Once in talking with a group of ceramics engineers about an exhibition of historic Chinese porcelains, I found these professional men were amazed that such variety and technical perfection could have been achieved without the resources of modern technology—no chemical analysis of materials and glazes, no pyrometers to measure the heat of the kiln, no scientifically controlled heating.

Trial and error were the method, and the thousands of "wasters" at ancient kiln sites are an indication of the enormous effort, the enormous losses that underlay success. There is a story about a potter named T'ung, so desperate over carrying out orders from the emperor for huge fish bowls that he leapt into the flames of the kiln. The bowls turned out perfectly.[2]

The shaping hands of an individual potter are so much a part of the ceramic tradition that we instinctively respond by wanting to take a bowl in our own hands, to turn it around in the light, to explore the surface with our fingers. Since this is impossible with the pieces reproduced here in photographs, or with ceramics in the glass cases of museums, you will have to imagine the process for yourself. But you can always give your hands and fingers some practice by closing them "feelingly" around an apple, a pear, an orange, or a green pepper. Close your eyes and let your fingers tell you the differences in texture of the fruit, or of a basket, a stone, the polished interior of a nutshell. To paraphrase a current advertising slogan, let your fingers do the talking; they will inform you. An awareness of such forms and textures has always been a part of the potter's experience.

We have tried to show in what ways the landscape paintings of China tell us about the attitudes of the scholar-artists toward nature, attitudes that are both poetic and philosophic. In ceramics the elements of nature itself—earth, air, water, and fire—interact with the simple human need for cups and bowls. There is something disarming about the way that potters everywhere have talked about their pots: the foot, the body, the belly, the shoulder, the neck, the mouth, the lip, as if pots somehow shared our human condition. To observe how these different parts of a pot are handled, whether with clear-cut differentiation of parts or with subtle, sometimes imperceptible, transitions, is one way of sensing differences of style and of period.

The lines of the *Tao te ch'ing* already quoted in Chapter 2 may very well be remembered here, and with specific meaning:

> Thirty spokes share the wheel's hub;
> It is the center hole that makes it useful.
> Shape clay into a vessel;
> It is the space within that makes it useful.

Our concern, then, is to attune ourselves to the space enclosed by the form, to the form itself, and to the treatment of surfaces. If the ceramic piece serves a useful purpose, does it really work? Is the surface glazed? Does the glaze suit the shape it covers, as the skin of a pear suits the pear? Does the ornament, if any, seem to belong to the character of the pot? It is interesting also to try to find out in what way the presence of local materials influenced the pottery centers, and how ideas from outside China have, from time to time, affected local craftsmen. Every time we use the familiar household word "china," we unconsciously pay tribute to the supreme skills of Chinese craftsmen, and to the long history of their art.

In the art of the potter, our lives and the lives of people in distant times and places can meet at a very human and everyday level. A Yuan-dynasty saucer in the Sir Percival David Collection in London is decorated with a molded design of five small boys, each holding in his hand a lotus blossom. They appear to be dancing around a central lotus leaf. Seeing this white *Ting* ware dish at a loan exhibition in this country and again in London, I remembered photographing children in the town of Ting Chou who were about to perform a traditional folk dance, each one holding a paper lantern in the shape of a lotus blossom. So apparently

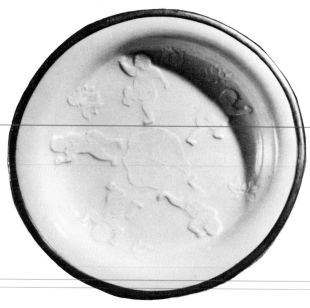

Saucer: Ting Ware 13th-14th century

Preparing for the Lotus Lantern Dance
Photograph by the author

a folk custom, impressed on that little dish six hundred years or more ago, had survived into the twentieth century. The town of Ting Chou (or Ting Hsien) in North China was the capital of a prefecture in which a Japanese scholar in 1941 found the kiln sites of that beautiful white ware so much admired in the Sung dynasty and by collectors of our own time.

One of the things that makes the study of Chinese ceramics so fascinating today is that new discoveries keep coming to light. In this century, fragments of Chinese pots have been found in excavations in the Near East, in Egypt, and in Japan, fragments that help to date some of the well-known wares. Chinese, Japanese, and European scholars have searched for and found important kiln sites in China, and whole ancient centers for the production of ceramics. And archaeologists in China, in the last few years, have pushed back the beginning of porcelain by a thousand years, as we shall see in a later chapter.

The illustrations that follow present eighteen objects from forty centuries, a small and very personal anthology consisting of six examples from Neolithic times through the T'ang and the Five dynasties, six from the Sung and the Yuan dynasties, and six from the Ming and the Ch'ing. A small sampling among a thousand treasures, they suggest something of the variety, style, inventiveness, and technical achievements of the Chinese potters. You will find pieces that appear proud and stern or small and endearing, subtly restrained or grandly imposing. Some of them incorporate borrowings from other cultures, but they are all, with the possible exception of the first and oldest piece, unmistakably and distinctively Chinese. If objects from the Cleveland Museum of Art outnumber others, it is because the writer knows them best—has been privileged to handle and touch some of the pieces. But all of them come from collections that are open to the public in the United States or in England. Many more may be studied with delight in Canada, in Europe, and in the Near East, in Japan, Taiwan, and in the People's Republic of China.

I
Neolithic Times (c. 7000–1750 B.C.) through the T'ang (A.D. 618–907) and Five Dynasties (907–960)

Even in the reproduction, it seems possible to sense the strength and spirited brushwork of this burial pot from the Neolithic period, discovered by the Swedish geologist J. G. Andersson in 1923 in what is now Kansu Province of northwestern China. (page 72, above left).

This rare and well-preserved Bronze Age jar from Anyang, of white unglazed earthenware, is carved with zigzag designs that recall the geometric patterns of the bronze ritual vessels. (page 72, above right).

One of the largest and most interesting ceramic pieces in this country from the Han dynasty (Eastern Han: A.D. 25–220) is a multiple-

Vase: Pan-shan type Neolithic period

Jar Shang dynasty

House Model Han dynasty

storied house model, more than four feet high, of painted pottery. There was space for the animals to be kept at night on the ground level, living quarters above, and a watch tower at the top. (page 72, below).

In the tombs of the T'ang dynasty, pottery representations of horses and servants had long since replaced the living sacrifices demanded by powerful nobles of a more primitive time. And in the T'ang dynasty, fine horses, important to the military, were greatly admired, and were brought at enormous cost from Western Asia. (Illustrated in color on page 86).

Horse T'ang dynasty

A proud and fierce ewer with its spout in the shape of a phoenix head incorporates some of the international contacts of the T'ang period. The lotus petals of the base are part of a motif that came with Buddhism from India, while the strongly designed ornamental bands are borrowed from the Sassanian culture of the Near East. The white porcelain of this late T'ang vase was to be developed and refined in later periods. (below, right)

Ewer with Phoenix-headed Spout
Late T'ang dynasty

Bowl: Yueh Ware Five Dynasties

Following the green glazed stonewares made in the Han dynasty, kilns south of the Yangtze developed what became known as *Yueh* ware. These gray-green, brownish, and olive-green wares preceded the famous celadons of the Sung dynasty. This bowl with its carved decoration of dragons chasing each other through the waves probably comes from the tenth century. (above, left)

Northern Sung (960–1127)
Southern Sung (1127–1279)
Yuan (1280–1368)

The next two pieces were made during the Northern Sung dynasty. (960–1127). The first is an elegant ivory-white conical bowl of *Ting* ware, with its freely incised rhythmical design of a pair of mandarin ducks, of reeds and combed waves. (below, left)

Conical Bowl: Ting Ware
Northern Sung dynasty

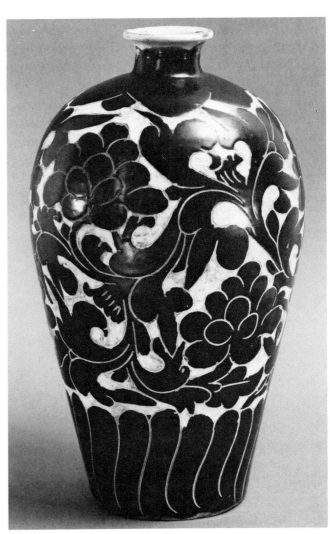

Vase: Tz'u-chou Ware
Northern Sung dynasty

The delicate *Ting* bowl may be said to represent an aristocratic taste; while the *mei p'ing* pot of Tz'u chou ware, intended to hold a flowering branch, may be said to represent a bolder folk tradition. Here a brownish-black slip, applied over the white slip, was carved to make the collar of stylized petals around the neck and the stylized leaves around the base. A thin white slip was brushed onto the spaces within the central design of peonies. (above, right)

Vase: Lung-ch'uan Ware
Sung dynasty

These are two examples of the imperial wares made during the sophisticated and elegant Southern Sung period, when the court had fled south to the beautiful city of Hangchou. A specialty of the geographical area of Hangchou was *Lung-ch'uan* ware with its thick jadelike celadon glaze in soft greens and blue-greens.

Incense Burner: Kuan Ware
Southern Sung dynasty

Even more restrained is the subtlety of the *Kuan* (imperial) ware incense burner. A thick glaze, still jadelike, but in more subdued gray-blue and brown-blue tones, flows over a very thin dark body. The glaze has a controlled crackle in which the delicate web of the fissures sometimes seems to accent the form of the vessel itself. (Illustrated in color on page 86).

Tea Bowl: Ch'ien Ware Sung dynasty

A third piece from the Southern Sung period is a small tea bowl known as *Ch'ien* ware in China and as *Temmoku* in Japan, made in the southern province of Fukien. It is dark to enrich the color of green tea and rather heavily potted to retain its warmth. The brown or purplish-brown glazes are sometimes streaked ("hare's fur") or spotted ("oil spot"). Much admired in Japan, these tea bowls were lovingly cherished for the tea ceremony.

The understated refinements of porcelain at the Southern Sung court were not to the taste of the Mongol conquerors who looked for something more obviously decorative. The most far-reaching innovation of the brief Yuan dynasty (1280–1368) was the introduction of cobalt blue applied to a

Covered Vase Yuan dynasty

white body and then covered with a transparent glaze. Known as "Mohammedan blue," because the color was at first imported from the Near East, the blue-and-white porcelains were made at Ching te chen in Kiangsi Province, not far from modern Shanghai. This ware for the next five hundred years was to be influential not only in China, but in Japan, the Near East, in Europe, and in the United States. (page 77, below).

III
Ming Dynasty (1368–1644)
Ch'ing Dynasty (1644–1912)

Plant forms in a landscape setting make up a single unified composition on the center of this early Ming dynasty blue-and-white plate. Set down with a fresh and graceful brush, we see the painterly skills that were to be characteristic of many Chinese porcelains from the fifteenth century on. (left)

Vase: Fa-hua type
Ming dynasty

Large Dish Ming dynasty

The *mei-p'ing* vase of a type known as *fa-hua* was made with little ridges of clay outlining the design (in this case the flowers and leaves of lotus form the main motif). Against a rich blue ground these outlined areas were filled, in imitation of cloisonné enamel, with pale yellow and blue areas, using also the white of the body. The effect is quite different from designs freely brushed on the pots in underglaze blue, and suggests the richness of cloisonné or of Chinese embroideries. (Illustrated in color on page 87).

The fifteenth-century wine cup, a small and endearing piece, less than two inches high is delicately outlined in underglaze blue and completed with overglaze enamels of greens, red, yellow, and pale violet. The technical achievement appears effortless, never suggesting the complexity of the process. (Illustrated in color on page 87).

Wine Cup Ming dynasty

In striking contrast to the little wine cup stands the great goldfish bowl, nearly two feet in diameter, made in the reign of the Ch'ing dynasty emperor and patron of the arts, K'ang-Hsi (1662–1722). The "five-color" decoration that represents a lotus pond so delightfully is painted in a group of colors—red, blue, yellow, purple, and various shades of green—known in the West by the French designation *famille verte.* The English scholar and connoisseur W. B. Honey has pointed out the unique quality of many ceramic colors which differ from the pigments used in painting on canvas or wood in that they are held in suspension in a glaze or glass which fills all inequalities of surface and "brings out the colour" as water does to pebbles in a rock-pool.

Bowl for Goldfish Ch'ing dynasty

Installation at Nelson Gallery-Atkins Museum, Kansas City

Pilgrim Vase: Lang Ware
Ch'ing dynasty

Vase of Enameled Porcelain
Ch'ing dynasty

Our designations for the monochrome glazes of the Ming and Ch'ing dynasties have a charm of their own—apple green, tea dust, oxblood, peach bloom, among others. Sometimes French designations have been used in the West—*clair de lune,* a soft blue; *famille verte, famille noire,* and *famille rose* for particular groups of colors. This oxblood or *lang* ware pilgrim flask, to use the Chinese name, made in the reign of K'ang Hsi, represents the technical brilliance that produced the monochrome glazes of the Ch'ing dynasty—green, blue, red, yellow, pale violet, pure white, and "mirror" black. (left)

And finally, here is a small vase from eighteenth-century China in which European influences are clear. Painted in the *famille rose* colors, it belongs to a small group of pots made to please the Ch'ien lung emperor. Said to have been brought from China more than a century ago by a correspondent of the *Times* of London in Peking, the vase was in his collection on a remote island off the Scottish coast. After his death, it was sent to England with other treasures but was lost in a shipwreck; years later the little vase was rescued from the sea. (right)

6
THE BRIDGE ON THE WILLOW PLATE

. . . spices, drugges, silks, calicos, quilts, carpets, and colours &c. The spices were pepper, cloves, maces, nutmegs, cinamon, greene ginger; the drugs were benjamin, frankincence, galingale, mirabolans, aloes, zocotrina, camphire; the silks damasks, taffetas, sarcenets, altobassos, that is, counterfeit cloth of gold, unwrought China silke, sleaved silke, white twisted silke, curled cypresse. The calicos were book-calicos, calico launes, broad white calicos, fine starched calicos, course white calicos, browne broad calicos, browne course calicos. There were also canopies and course diaper towels, quilts of course sarcenet and of calico, carpets like those from Turkey; whereunto are to be added the pearle, muske, civet and ambergriece. The rest of the wares were many in number but less in value; as elephants' teeth, porcellan vessels of China, coco-nuts, hides, ebenwood as black as jet, bedsteads of the same, cloth of the rinds of trees very strange for the matter, and artificiall in workmanship. All which piles of commodities being by men of approved judgement rated but in reasonable sort amounted to no less than 150000 li. sterling which being divided among the adventurers (whereof her Majesty was the chiefe) was sufficient to yield contentment to all parties.[1]

This fragrant and exotic cargo was unloaded at Dartmouth on the English Channel from a huge Spanish carrack, or merchant ship, the *Madre de Dios,* captured on her return voyage from the Far East by bold sailors of Queen Elizabeth's fleet. The year was 1592, only four years after the defeat of the Spanish Armada. It is just possible that the queen kept for herself some of the Chinese porcelain, since it was greatly prized by the rulers of Europe and pieces are known to have been in her possession. King Philip II of Spain took pride in his own enormous collection.

It is said that the first piece of Chinese porcelain to reach Europe was brought back by Marco Polo (1254–1324), a piece still preserved in the Museum of San Marco in Venice. In a detail of the painting *Feast of the*

Giovanni Bellini *Feast of the Gods,* Italian (detail)

Gods by Giovanni Bellini, the drinking vessel is a Ming porcelain blue and white bowl, probably copied from those presented to the doges of Venice by sultans of Egypt (illustrated also on page 270).

These and other contacts of the Italians with the Far East make it seem natural that the first attempts to imitate Chinese porcelain in Europe were made in Florence for a Medici grand duke. But the secret of this hard and gleaming ware could not easily be found out, although the white "Medici" ware was decorated with elegant designs in blue that acknowledged their Chinese source. A short-lived experiment had failed.

Medici Plate Italian

By the middle of the seventeenth century, great quantities of porcelain were being shipped out of Canton, first in Portuguese ships, later in Spanish, Dutch, and English vessels to Europe. These attractive bowls and plates, or local copies of them may be observed in Dutch paintings, still lifes and interiors, of the seventeenth century. Note the porcelain bowl in the still life on page 85. In Delft, in Holland, a thriving business developed in the manufacture of pottery (earthenware which has not the hardness of true porcelain) with overglaze blue decoration patterned after Chinese models. In France and in England, strenuous efforts were made to arrive at porcelain, but the precise ingredients used by the Chinese could not be determined.

The ruler who was most interested in finding the secret of porcelain was a German, Augustus the Strong, of Saxony. He was such a passionate collector of porcelain that he is said to have exchanged a regiment of dragoons for forty-eight blue-and-white vases. He had in his employ an alchemist named Böttger who had been thrown in jail for failing to turn common metals into gold. On coming out of jail, he set to work to find the true ingredients of porcelain. In 1710, Böttger produced a dark red stoneware so hard that it could be carved and polished like semiprecious stones. Not long after, a white porcelain was developed, known thereafter as hard-paste porcelain. Augustus the Strong then announced the opening of the Royal Porcelain Manufacture at Meissen near Dresden, where trade secrets were carefully guarded. Colored glazes were developed; skilled painters were employed. In the middle of the eighteenth century, talented modelers were employed to specialize in the making of figures, birds, and animals, often "in the Chinese style." Great table services were produced for the nobility, sometimes decorated with Chinese motifs and sometimes with adaptations of Japanese designs.

Höchst Group: Chinese Emperor German

Abraham van Beyeren *Still Life with a Silver Wine Jar and a Reflected Portrait of the Artist at his Easel* Dutch

Horse T'ang dynasty
(see also page 73)

Incense Burner: Kuan Ware
Southern Sung dynasty
(see also page 76)

Vase: Fa-hua type Ming dynasty
(see also page 78)

Wine Cup Ming dynasty
(see also page 79)

Canton Mug and Plate Chinese export porcelain

Willow Plate English

Trade secrets could not long be kept. Soon the great ceramic centers of France at Vincennes and Sevres, encouraged by the court of Louis XV, were turning out porcelains in the elegant, lighthearted, assymmetrical style known as rococo. Textiles, costume, furniture, architecture, as well as ceramics, reflected the fashion, the mania, for Oriental motifs as interpreted by European artists. *Chinoiseries* is the French name used to describe these fantasies of the European eighteenth century.

In England, many centers of ceramic production began to produce wares in pottery and in "bone china," often decorated in what was considered to be the Chinese taste. Toward the end of the eighteenth century, the familiar Willow pattern came into being, probably adapted from the "Canton" ware that was exported from China. Reinvented into an English design, the pattern was in turn copied by the Chinese for export. Any child who ever scraped a willow plate with a teaspoon has the pattern indelibly stamped on his or her mind, especially the little bridge with the three figures stepping across, and the two birds overhead. Nursery rhymes and legends were composed in England to go with the pictures. The contemporary American poet James Merrill writes about the familiar pattern in "Willowware Cup" from which these lines are taken:

> Plum in bloom, pagoda, blue birds, plume of willow—
> Almost the replica of a prewar pattern—
>
> The same boat bearing the gnat-sized lovers away,
> The old bridge now bent double where her father signals
>
> Feebly, as from flypaper, minding less and less.
> Two smaller retainers with lanterns light him home.

Porcelain Plate, Sèvres French

Is that a scroll he carries? He must by now be immensely
Wise, and have given up earthly attachments, and all that.
*   *   *
But this lone, chipped vessel, if it fills,
Fills for you with something warm and clear.

Around its inner horizon the old odd designs
Crowd as before, and seem to concentrate on you.

They represent, I fancy, a version of heaven
In its day more trouble to mend than to replace:

Steep roofs aslant, minutely tiled;
Tilted honeycombs, thunderhead blue.[2]

Tea was not mentioned by Hakluyt in the varied cargo from the East
salvaged from the Spanish ship in Queen Elizabeth's day. But the East
India Company, which had been chartered in 1600, sent a gift to Charles
II of thirty-four ounces of tea in 1640. Within another thirty years, the
average annual export of tea from Canton to England had grown to a
million pounds a year, so great was the appeal of the "cup that cheers but
not inebriates." The demand for teacups and teapots was also a factor in
the import and manufacture of chinaware.

American colonists were forced by British law to buy anything
exported from the Orient through England. It was tea of the East India
Company that was tossed into Boston Harbor in 1773, a signal for the
approach of revolution. As soon as the war was over, enterprising
merchants and shipmasters from Boston, Salem, New York, and Phila-

delphia began competing for the wealth to be earned in trade with Canton, the only port, except for the Portuguese base in Macao, where Westerners were allowed to make contact with Chinese merchants.

Late in the eighteenth and early in the nineteenth century, Lin Yan-ken selected merchandise for J. S. Waln. Amber, alumroot, beeswax, and cassia lignea. Cinnabar, chinaware, chessmen carved from ivory tusks, and an elbowchair of rosewood. Embroidered fans, grass cloth, ginger in earthen pots. Hemp and indigo. Jute, kaolin, also lily flowers. Musk, nankeens, orpiment, a miniature pagoda of silver, and medicinal rhubarb. Packets of seeds of the melon and of the apricot. Teas, both green and black. Umbrellas, vases, and wall papers with scenes from Chinese life. Writer's ink and xanthein.

These are some of the items neatly entered in a time-yellowed account book, as sent by the Confucian merchant, from Canton in the ancient Empire of China, on sailing ships to the Quaker merchant in Philadelphia, U.S.A.

It is recorded, here at the Ancestral Hall of the Lin homestead, that Lin Yan-ken went to Canton and joined the business of his maternal uncle, Houqua, one of the thirteen men appointed by Ch'ien Lung, then Emperor of China, to trade with foreigners. He arrived on the day following the Festival of the Washing of Flowers, in the Year of the Pig, of the Chi-hai Cycle. He served there until the Dragon Boat Festival, in the Year of the Horse, of the Jen-wu Cycle. By Western calendar, from May 1779 to June 1822.[3]

These are the opening paragraphs of a book called *The House of Exile,* written in 1933 by a young woman from Philadelphia, Nora Waln, while visiting the patriarchal Chinese family who had kept alive the memory of the American merchant with whom an ancestor had once done business. The list of goods shipped is not unlike Hakluyt's account of the cargo in the Spanish ship captured by the English two hundred years earlier.

One of the remarkable aspects of the China trade in the United States is the youth of the captains and crews of the ships that made the long and dangerous voyages to China, sailing westward around Cape Horn (long before the Panama Canal was imagined), or eastward around the Cape of Good Hope and across the Indian Ocean. John Boit, Jr., at the age of nineteen, sailed as master of a sixty-foot sloop with a crew of twenty-two, out of Boston harbor on August 1, 1794. They went first to the northwest coast to buy furs for exchange in Canton. After a final skirmish with the Indians, they crossed the Pacific, arriving in Canton on December 5. Returning the other way around the world, Captain Boit, after many adventures, entered Boston harbor with his cargo on July 8, 1795.

The variety and intricacy of the cargoes were incredible, and often included detailed shopping lists from the ladies of Boston and Salem.

Attributed to Lam Qua *Houqua*

Gentlefolk in America, as in England and on the Continent, could send a drawing of their own coats of arms to Canton with instructions as to color and design. A year or more later they received a handsome set of custom-made porcelain tableware. The porcelain decorator followed so precisely the instructions given that occasionally the written notes in pencil, "red," "blue," "green," were reproduced exactly in the finished product.

This writer remembers with pleasure the festive look of the Thanksgiving dinner table in the home of New England cousins who had inherited a huge service from a Salem ship-captain ancestor. It was the Fitzhugh pattern in a golden orange with the great seal of the United

Extension Chair Chinese

Punch Bowl
Chinese export porcelain

"Fitzhugh" Pattern Group
Chinese export porcelain

States in brownish-black in the center of each piece, the rusty orange harmonizing with the cider-filled glasses all the way around a table set for as many as sixteen or twenty.

Western merchants engaged in the China trade in Canton were confined to a narrow strip of warehouses and offices along the quays. They were not permitted to enter the city itself. Wives and children who ventured to the Far East had to live in the Portuguese base at Macao, and were not permitted to set foot in the offices at Canton. Family letters, published and unpublished, tell a story of enterprise, of courage, of affection, of hardship, and often of great financial reward.

By the second quarter of the nineteenth century, American merchants were complaining that the quality of imported goods, even the skills of packing were deteriorating. The great days of the China trade would soon be over. The Chinese exhibition at the Centennial Exhibition in Philadelphia in 1876 may have been its last stand.

The bridge on the willow plate no longer invites us into a world of fantasy, the dream of China that enchanted those people of earlier times. The sailing ships with the beautiful names—the *Columbia,* the *Grand Turk,* the *Flying Cloud,* the *Sovereign of the Seas*—gave way to the steamers, and the steamers in turn have given way to the jet planes. In travel time, the Far East is not nearly so far as it once was.

Kuang
Early Western Chou dynasty

7

RECENT ARCHAEOLOGICAL DISCOVERIES

To come in contact with recent archaeology in China, with the fabulous treasures that have been brought to light since 1949, is to come in contact also with some basic ideas of the People's Republic of China.

At one time or another, the Chinese have looked back to a Golden Age, to the mythical kings at the dawn of history, to the time of Confucius, or to the stirring days of the Han dynasty (the Chinese call themselves the "Sons of Han"). But recent archaeology and modern ideology now converge on a time earlier than any of these, on the Neolithic age. One of the showplaces for modern archaeology is a village

94

called Pan-p'o in Shensi Province, to the west of the great bend in the Yellow River. There a large section of a prehistoric Stone Age village has been excavated, roofed over, provided with walkways and informative signboards. In Chinese thought today, the Neolithic period is seen as the new Golden Age when communal living was practiced without class divisions or class exploitation. From Pan-p'o, and from other Neolithic sites to the northwest, have come the red-clay vessels, painted or incised, that announce the incomparable skills of the Chinese potters for the next five or six thousand years. A shallow bowl from Pan-p'o, seventeen inches in diameter, dates from somewhere between 5000 B.C. and 3000 B.C. Painted with a curious human mask and two fishes, rather "as if they were whispering in its ears," this just may be the earliest representation of a human face in all of Chinese art.

Turning to the Bronze Age (roughly 1600–600 B.C.), which follows the Neolithic period, scholars had found it extraordinary that the ancient bronze vessels, so powerful in their expressive forms, so brilliant in their casting techniques, should have been known only at such a very accomplished level. No primitive beginnings of the art had hitherto come to light.

The ritual bronzes that survive from the Shang (1750–1111 B.C.) and Chou (1111–221 B.C.) dynasties are in fact a part of Chinese history,

Painted Basin Neolithic period

symbolizing the effort to honor and appease the spirits of the ancestors through sacrifices of food and wine. Sometimes inscriptions recorded bits of historical information. The inscribed characters, cast in bronze, are themselves the ancestors of Chinese writing today.

One of the accomplishments of modern archaeology has been to explore in detail two capitals of the almost mythical Shang dynasty: a late capital excavated at Anyang in 1934, and an earlier capital (perhaps Ao) found under the city of Chengchow, just south of the Yellow River, along with other more primitive sites.

The ceramic water or wine vessel, *tsun,* on page 106 found at Chengchow, is a high-fired stoneware; it is fully glazed, to the amazement of scholars in China and in the West. Very close to a true porcelain, it sets back the date of the discovery of porcelaneous stoneware in China by a thousand years. It represents a point of technical knowledge that was not reached in Europe, as we have seen, until the eighteenth century A.D.

Since the ancient bronze vessels of China are now known to have been cast in clay molds, known as "piece molds," it is obvious that a high degree of technical skill in ceramics was necessary to create a formula for a clay that could withstand the heat of the molten metal. In later ages, when the bronze vessels were no longer made, their characteristic forms were remembered and honored in beautiful examples of the potter's art.

The shape of the ceramic pot illustrated may be compared with a bronze ritual wine vessel on page 107, also found at Chengchow. An evil-averting monster mask called the *T'ao-t'ieh,* with its two eyes, two horns, and snout or nose, is expressed here in a fairly simple form. But the mask was to reappear with variations and complications for many centuries.

The Han dynasty (202 B.C.–220 A.D.) was a period of great energy, of geographical expansion, and, among wealthy people and the ruling families, a time of intense concern with burial customs. In 1972 at Ma-wang-tui outside of Ch'angsha, south of the Yangtze River, at a site where hospital construction was planned, a tomb was found, carefully excavated, and reported. It turned out to be the tomb of the wife of a marquess of Tai, in the ancient state of Ch'u. The event was sensational in two ways; first, for the astonishing state of preservation of the lady; and second, and more important, for the beauty and significance of the objects buried with her in the belief that she could enjoy them in the afterlife.

Sixty feet beneath the burial mound, packed in a layer of moist, white clay and layers of moisture-absorbing charcoal, inside of one enclosing coffin after another, wrapped in many garments of delicate silk was the body of the lady herself. This was no dried mummy, as in Egypt; the flesh was still moist, the joints movable, the long black hair in place. An autopsy determined that she had type-A blood, that she had borne a number of children, that there were signs of tuberculosis in the left lung, and that just before her death she had eaten 138 melon seeds. How long had she lain there? More than two thousand years. She was buried about the year 180 B.C.

Superb, brilliantly-colored lacquer pieces were found in the tomb, including dishes with chopsticks on a tray, and food of every kind—chicken, fish, rice, eggs, strawberries, and fruits. There were musical instruments, intricate textiles, costumes of silk gauze for summer, wadded and embroidered ones for winter, cosmetics, and a wig, along with 162 wooden figurines of attendants and musicians.

Laid under the lid of the innermost coffin (a work of art in itself) was the painted banner of extraordinary interest, illustrated on page 108. It was a painting on silk in the form of the familiar hanging scroll except for a slightly wider section at the top. Creatures of the lower world, of the earth—probably the lady herself richly dressed, with her attendants—and of the heavens are represented. The moon and the sun are in the upper left and right corners. Some sense of the beliefs expressed by the symbols painted on the banner, and of the reasons for the lavish furnishing of the tomb may be gained by reading a long poem, "The Summons of the Soul," one of the *Songs of Ch'u,* from which a passage is quoted in the next section, " A Literary Interlude," page 114.

Before World War II, I made the journey a number of times on the Peking-Hankow railway southward from Peking to the towns of Ting Hsien and also to Pao Ting in Hopei Province. A golden afternoon light always seemed to be slanting across the level fields. Beyond the fields, to the west, were blue-violet hills with their rugged and changing profile, a continuous panorama. One could distinguish no towns in the hills, no landmarks, and I often wondered, pressing my nose against the glass of the railway-car window, what secrets were hidden there.

In 1968, apparently in the course of some defense construction, soldiers came upon what turned out to be huge tombs cut deep into the solid rock of a hillside at Man-ch'eng, about ninety miles south of Peking, somewhere in those blue-violet hills west of the railroad. The entrance had been secured by pouring molten iron between walls of brick. The passages, side chambers, and main hall were crowded with objects, many of them of extraordinary beauty, both of materials and of workmanship. Twenty-eight hundred objects made up the treasure found in the adjoining tombs of Princess Tou Wan and her husband, the Prince Liu Sheng who died in 113 B.C., brother of the Emperor Wu. Photographs of the spectacular "jade suits" that encased the prince and the princess were much reproduced at the time of the important exhibition of "Archaeological Finds from China" shown in Europe in 1973, and later, in Toronto, Washington, and Kansas City. Thin rectangular tablets of jade—2,160 of them—sewed together with gold thread encased the princess. Jade had always been believed to have magical properties; the Taoist magicians who were influential at that time believed that jade would prevent decay of the corpses. Both suits had collapsed, but could be completely reconstructed.

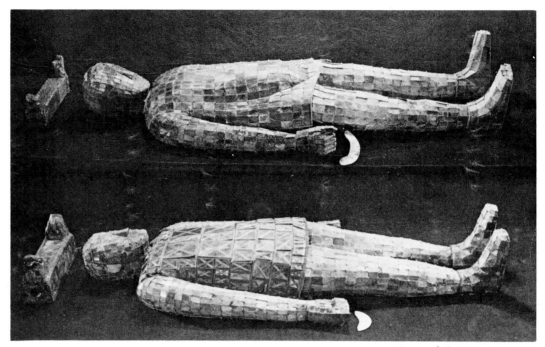

Funeral Suits c. 113 B.C.

*Lantern in the Form
of a Kneeling Girl
c. 113 B.C.*

If the jade suits were the most spectacular finds at Man-ch'eng, some of the other finds were more truly beautiful. The most touching, the most moving object found is a bronze lantern in the shape of a serving girl, so arranged that the direction of the light may be adjusted, and that smoke will be carried off through her sleeve. The inscription reads, "Eternal Fidelity." The lantern is both a useful object and, in the kneeling girl, an impressive sculpture.

Flying Horse
later Han dynasty

No one who saw the exhibition of which we have just spoken will forget the "flying horse," one of 177 bronze objects found in a tomb of the second century A.D. in the far northwest, in Kansu Province. There had been two robberies of this tomb of a Chinese general in ancient times, but a procession of horse carriages, drivers, and attendants remained, along with the famous horse. He is lightly touching the back of a swallow with his right hind hoof, perhaps as an indication that he was truly flying, perhaps because his name may have been "Flying Swallow." Notice especially the expressive head, neighing as he goes galloping into the wind.

In this small selection from among thousands of sites excavated, in the last twenty-five years, we have chosen, for its wall paintings and ceramic figures, the tomb of the Princess Yung T'ai, dated A.D. 706, in the brilliant time of the T'ang dynasty. The princess died at the age of eighteen or nineteen, in childbirth, according to the epitaph, although she may have been forced by her terrible grandmother, the Empress Wu, to hang herself. After the grandmother died, her father became emperor, and arranged for the splendid reburial of his daughter and her husband. The tomb is in Shensi Province to the west of the T'ang capital, Ch'ang-an (now Sian). Although they were never meant to be seen again, the tomb figurines of glazed ceramic, known in Chinese as *ming ch'i,* are here especially lively and accomplished—musicians, ladies of the court, hunters, polo players, horses, among many others.

Huntsman and Cheetah
T'ang dynasty

Frescolike paintings on the wall of the antechamber of the tomb are charming in themselves, and important for the history of art. Attendants of the princess come carrying objects for her use and pleasure—a fan, a candle, boxes, perhaps of sweets or of cosmetics, and what may be bundles of silks. It is clear that the attendants are young ladies of fashion, in their high-waisted gowns and long stoles. Represented within the setting of the palace, they are more individual, informal, more youthful, than the stately attendants of the empress, carved in flowing and voluminous robes, two hundred years earlier, on the walls of the cave-chapel at Lung-men (see illustrations, page 35). Since so little survives from paintings of the eighth century, it is a matter for rejoicing that these murals, masterful if sketchy, have survived in the tomb of Princess Yung-T'ai.

Section of a Mural Painting
T'ang dynasty

Attendant of the
Princess Yung-t'ai (detail)

In 1974, a little to the east of Ch'ang-an (modern Sian, capital of Shensi province in Northwest China) commune peasants were digging wells looking for water. They were close to a great mound that rises above the tomb of Ch'in Shih Huang Ti, the first emperor and unifier of China who died in 210 B.C. In a rectangular area of three acres, an extraordinary underground army of pottery warriors is gradually emerging. By September 1976 it was reported that 580 life-size clay warriors and 24 life-size clay horses had emerged.[1] It is now estimated that when completely excavated as many as 6,000 figures may be found. They were not made in molds, but as individual sculptures, varied in facial type and in dress. Some of the soldiers carried actual bronze weapons. As they were lined up in rows, the array of figures indicates how a Chinese army was organized, two thousand years ago.

Since the founding of the People's Republic of China, archaeological work has been guided by Mao Tse-tung's policy of "making the past serve the present." Emphasis in presenting these objects, in their own museums, or in traveling exhibits, is on what they represent as social history, demonstrating the exploitation of the masses or the cruelty and extravagance of the ruling classes. The almost miraculous skills of the craftsmen are rightly praised. There are, of course, no kind words for the taste and aesthetic perceptions of their patrons. But in the West, at least, lavish expenditure and diligent work do not automatically produce great works of art.

Visitors to the museums in China in which these objects and those from older collections are displayed are dismayed to find few scroll paintings, few ink paintings, on exhibition except in Peking. Barbara Tuchman remarked that the supreme painting of old China is one form of art that cannot by any stretch of the dialectic be represented as a product of the masses, and is therefore very little exhibited, if at all.[2] Chinese painting is, however, carefully stored and preserved.

What recent archaeology has proved is important in a number of ways. It has confirmed the legendary history of the Shang dynasty, and has shown that the culture of ancient China had a much wider geographical spread than had previously been realized. And it has demonstrated the existence of porcelaneous stoneware, of "almost porcelain," a thousand years earlier than anyone supposed.

Finally, it should be pointed out that all this has been what is known as "salvage archaeology," discoveries made in the course of building highways and dams, of looking for water, of constructing airports and industrial sites. Who knows what treasures may be found when there is time and money for "purposeful archaeology"?

Excavating Horses and Warriors Photograph

Head of a Warrior Photograph

Warrior Figure Photograph

Lacquer Jar with Lid c. 180 B.C.

Water or Wine Vessel: Ts'un
Shang dynasty

Wine Vessel: Ts'un Shang dynasty

Painted Banner c. 180 B.C.

A Literary Interlude

白雲如帶東山腰石
磴飛空細路遙欄倚
杖藜舒眺望欲因鳴
澗谷吹簫 沈周

Shen Chou *Poet on a Mountain*

8
CHINA

The use of literature
Lies in its conveyance of every truth.
It expands the horizon to make space infinite,
And serves as a bridge that spans a myriad years.
It maps all roads and paths for posterity,
And mirrors the images of worthy ancients,
That the tottering Edifices of the sage kings of antiquity may be reared
* again,*
And their admonishing voices, wind-borne since of yore, may resume
* full expression.*
No regions are too remote but it pervades,
No truth too subtle to be woven into its vast web.
Like mist and rain, it permeates and nourishes,

And manifests all the powers of transformation in which gods and
spirits share.
Virtue it makes endure and radiate on brass and stone,
And resound in an eternal stream of melodies ever renewed on pipes and
strings.[1]

Poetry, Robert Frost observed, is what gets lost in translation. Once, traveling at night on the Peking-Hankow railway—no electric lights in our car, just a candle or two—I was listening to an intense conversation among a group of Chinese friends. A writer brought up the problem of translation. In an offhand way I asked why he didn't translate John Milton, just for something really easy, and began to recite:

"Adam, the goodliest man of men since born
His sons; the fairest of her daughters, Eve,
Under a tuft of shade, that on a green
Stood whispering soft, by a fresh fountain-side
They sat them down."[2]

I still remember exactly the words of his prompt reply: "If I should translate John Milton, there would be a Paradise quite lost."

Chinese poetry in English translation was not readily accessible to the general public until this century. Around 1910, poets of the Imagist Movement, found something in translations from Chinese and Japanese that influenced their writing in somewhat the same way that painters in France had been influenced, in the late nineteenth century, by Japanese prints. Ezra Pound published a little book of translations called *Cathay* in 1915; Arthur Waley his *170 Poems from the Chinese* in 1918. Arthur Waley, an Englishman, a brilliant scholar and translator, taught himself Chinese and Japanese while working in the Print Department of the British Museum. The American poet, Ezra Pound, had to work from English translations of Japanese translations of Chinese poems, but he had an ear for the rhythms of English speech which gave his renderings a special charm. In the last twenty-five years, Chinese, English, and American scholars have been busy translating and publishing, often in paperback, so that a wide range of poetry and prose is now available to us in English.

Chinese poetry rhymes and has an intricate pattern of tones within lines of strict length, often of five or seven characters. Poems that translate best are those that depend on vivid visual images or lively figures of speech. Verse that depends on musical quality, or on a wealth of literary and historical allusions, is lost to us. But just as we can admire the ink paintings without being able to analyze brushstrokes, we can, I think, in the best translations, delight in the poems without, alas, being able to read the characters. What follows, then, is a brief sampling out of all of Chinese poetry from two early collections, and from six major poets.

It is hard to realize that some of the poems in the *Book of Songs,* also called the *Book of Poetry,* go back to the time of the Chou bronzes. This, the oldest collection of Chinese poetry, is said to have been compiled by Confucius around 600 B.C. although many poems are thought to be much older. According to one Western scholar, the verses, read in Chinese, are often charged with the greatest "beauty, fire, and delicacy."

The three short poems that follow are from the three hundred or so in the *Book of Songs.* They have to do with courtship and marriage, with court ceremonies, and with seedtime and harvest, three groups into which many of the poems seem to fall.

Plop fall the plums; but there are still seven.
Let those gentlemen that would court me
Come while it is lucky!

Plop fall the plums; there are still three.
Let any gentleman that would court me
Come before it is too late!

Plop fall the plums; in shallow baskets we lay them.
Any gentleman who would court me
Had better speak while there is time.[3]

How goes the night?
Midnight has still to come.
Down in the court the torch is blazing bright;
I hear far off the throbbing of the drum.

How goes the night?
The night is not yet gone.
I hear the trumpets blowing on the height;
The torch is paling in the coming dawn.

How goes the night?
The night is past and done.
The torch is smoking in the morning light,
The dragon banner floating in the sun.[4]

Speed, speed the plow
on south slopes now
grain is to sow
        lively within.

Here come your kin,
baskets round
baskets square,
millet's there.

With a crowd of rain-hats
and clicking hoes
out goes the weed
to mulch and rot
on dry and wet,
crop will be thicker on that spot.

Harvest high,
reapers come by
so they mow
to heap it like a wall
comb-tooth'd and tall

an hundred barns to fill
till wives and childer fear no ill.

At harvest home kill a yellow bull,
by his curved horn is luck in full
(be he black-nosed seven foot high,
so tall's felicity).

Thus did
men of old
who left us this land
to have and to hold.[5]

The poems in the *Book of Songs* were made by people of the Yellow River valley. The next important collection comes from the Yangtze River valley to the south, from the state of Ch'u, in the fourth and third centuries B.C. In the lines quoted here from "The Summons of the Soul," a shaman, or priest, tries to recall a dying king to the life he has known in the land of Ch'u. Although earlier in date than the recently excavated tomb of Lady Tai at Ma-wang-tui (see page 96), details of furnishings and textiles suggest the kind of luxury with which her family hoped to provide her in the afterlife.

O soul, come back! and enter the gate of the city.
The priests are there who call you, walking backwards to lead you in.
Ch'in basket-work, silk cords of Ch'i, and silken banners of Cheng:
All things are there proper for your recall; and with long-drawn,
   piercing cries they summon the wandering soul.
O soul, come back! Return to your old abode.
All the quarters of the world are full of harm and evil.
Hear while I describe for you your quiet and reposeful home.
High halls and deep chambers, with railings and tiered balconies;
Stepped terraces, storied pavilions, whose tops look on the high
   mountains;

Lattice doors with scarlet interstices, and carving on the square lintels;
Draughtless rooms for winter; galleries cool in summer;
Streams and gullies wind in and out, purling prettily;
A warm breeze bends the melilotus and sets the tall orchids swaying.
Crossing the hall into the apartments, the ceilings and floors are vermilion,
The chambers of polished stone, with kingfisher hangings on jasper hooks;
Bedspreads of kingfisher seeded with pearls, all dazzling in brightness;
Arras of fine silk covers the walls; damask canopies stretch overhead,
Braids and ribbons, brocades and satins, fastened with rings of precious stone.
Many a rare and precious thing is to be seen in the furnishings of the chamber.[6]

There are magical and erotic overtones in the *Songs of Ch'u,* and rich visual images. The poet, Ch'u Yuan is the first identifiable individual poet in Chinese literature. The imaginary portrait reproduced on page 116 was painted a thousand years later. Here are two brief excerpts from the *Nine Songs:*

> In his fish-scale house, dragon-scale hall,
> Portico of purple-shell, in his red palace,
> What is the Spirit doing, down in the water?
> Riding a white turtle, followed by stripy fish
> With you I wandered in the islands of the River.
> The ice is on the move; soon the floods will be down.
> You salute me with raised hands, then go towards the East.
> I go with my lovely one as far as the southern shore.
> The waves surge on surge come to meet him,
> Fishes shoal after shoal escort me on my homeward way.[7]

> The rites are accomplished to the beating of the drums;
> The flower-wand is passed on to succeeding dancers.
> Lovely maidens sing their song, slow and solemnly.
> Orchids in spring and chrysanthemums in autumn:
> So it shall go on until the end of time.[8]

The poet of the *Nine Songs* is a legendary character. But T'ao Ch'ien (also called T'ao Yuan-Ming), who lived from A.D. 365–427, is very real as you can see even in the imaginary portrait on page 117 by a quirky artist of the seventeenth century. The poet loved the fragrance of the chrysan-

Chang Wu *Imaginary Portrait of Ch'u Yuan*

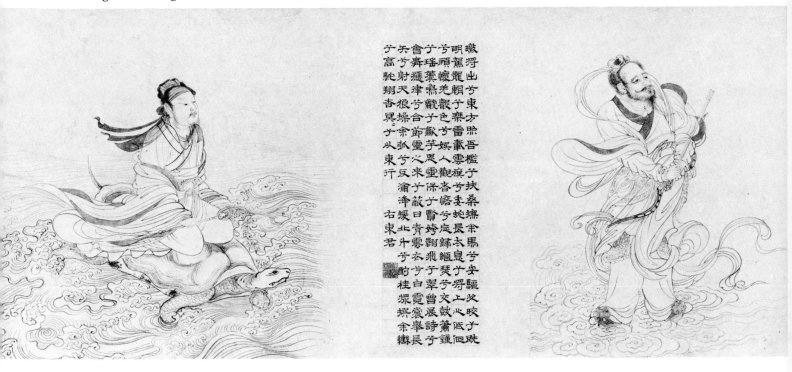

嗷浮出兮東方照吾檻兮扶桑撫余馬兮安驅夜皎皎兮既明駕龍輈兮乘雷載雲旗兮委蛇長太息兮將上心低佪兮顧懷羌色娛人兮觀者憺兮忘歸亙瑟兮交鼓簫鍾兮瑤簴鳴籂兮吹竽思靈保兮賢姱翾飛兮翠曾展詩兮會舞應律兮合節靈之來兮蔽日青雲衣兮白霓裳舉長矢兮射天狼操余弧兮反淪援北斗兮酌桂漿撰余轡兮高馳翔杳冥兮以東行右東君

themums, music (his lute is beside him), and the wine that is in the crockery jar at the lower right, complete with dipper and cup. He is often quoted by later poets. Two of his poems have been the subject of innumerable paintings.

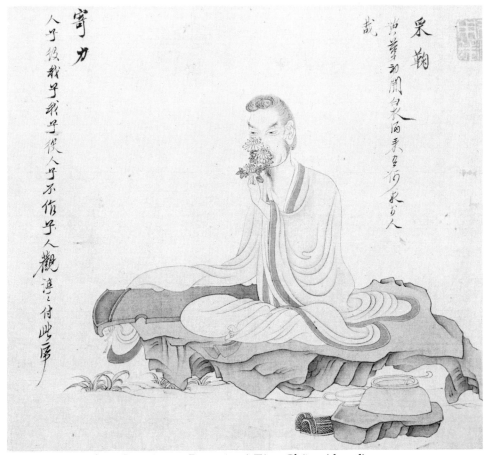

Ch'en Hung-shou *Imaginary Portrait of T'ao Ch'ien* (detail)

This is the first of five poems on returning to dwell in the country:

In youth I had nothing
    that matched the vulgar tone,
For my nature always
    loved the hills and mountains.
Inadvertently I fell
    Into the Dusty Net [i.e., the world],
Once having gone
    it was more than thirteen years.
The tame bird
    longs for his old forest—
The fish in the house-pond
    thinks of his ancient pool.
I too will break the soil
    at the edge of the Southern moor,
I will guard simplicity
    and return to my fields and garden.
My land and house—
    a little more than ten acres,
In the thatched cottage—
    only eight or nine rooms.
Elms and willows
    shade the back verandah,
Peach and plum trees
    in rows before the hall.

Yao T'ing-mei *Leisure Enough to Spare* (detail)

Hazy and dimly seen
  a village in the distance,
Close in the foreground
  the smoke of neighbours' houses.
A dog barks
  amidst the deep lanes,
A cock is crowing
  atop a mulberry tree.
No dust and confusion
  within my doors and courtyard;
In the empty rooms,
  more than sufficient leisure.
Too long I was held
  within the barred cage.
Now I am able
  to return again to Nature.[9]

In almost every collection of Chinese paintings can be found at least one painting that derives its subject from the story of the Peach-blossom Spring. The paintings are always more interesting when one can see which aspects of the story the artist has selected for his composition.

During the reign-period T'ai yuan [326–97] of the Chin dynasty there lived in Wu-ling a certain fisherman. One day, as he followed the course of a stream, he became unconscious of the distance he had travelled. All at once he came upon a grove of blossoming peach trees which lined either bank for hundreds of paces. No tree of any other kind stood amongst them, but there were fragrant flowers, delicate and lovely to the eye, and the air was filled with drifting peachbloom.

The fisherman, marvelling, passed on to discover where the grove would end. It ended at a spring; and then there came a hill. In the side of the hill was a small opening which seemed to promise a gleam of light. The fisherman left his boat and entered the opening. It was almost too cramped at first to afford him passage; but when he had taken a few dozen steps he emerged into the open light of day. He faced a spread of level land. Imposing buildings stood among rich fields and pleasant ponds all set with mulberry and willow. Linking paths led everywhere, and the fowls and dogs of one farm could be heard from the next. People were coming and going and working in the fields. Both the men and the women dressed in exactly the same manner as people outside; white-haired elders and tufted children alike were cheerful and contented.

Some, noticing the fisherman, started in great surprise and asked him where he had come from. He told them his story. They then invited him to their home, where they set out wine and killed

Tao-Chi *The Peach-blossom Spring*

chickens for a feast. When news of his coming spread through the village everyone came in to question him. For their part they told how their forefathers, fleeing from the troubles of the age of Ch'in, had come with their wives and neighbours to this isolated place, never to leave it. From that time on they had been cut off from the outside world. They asked what age was this: they had never even heard of the Han, let alone its successors the Wei and the Chin. The fisherman answered each of their questions in full, and they sighed and wondered at what he had to tell. The rest all invited him to their homes in turn, and in each house food and wine were set before him. It was only after a stay of several days that he took his leave.

"Do not speak of us to the people outside," they said. But when he had regained his boat and was retracing his original route, he marked it at point after point; and on reaching the prefecture he sought audience of the prefect and told him of all these things. The prefect immediately despatched officers to go back with the fisherman. He hunted for the marks he had made, but grew confused and never found the way again.

The learned and virtuous hermit Liu Tzu-chi heard the story and
went off elated to find the place. But he had no success, and died at
length of a sickness. Since that time there have been no further
"seekers of the ford."[10]   T'AO CH'IEN

It is the story of a lost Golden Age—perhaps the poet is really saying that
you can't go home again.

It was in China's classic age, the T'ang dynasty (618–907), that the
empire reached its greatest extent, a time described by a French historian
as *la Chine joyeuse.* There was a great flowering of poetry—an
eighteenth-century anthology of T'ang verse collected 48,000 poems by
220 poets.

Two of China's greatest poets, Li Po and Tu Fu, were born close to
the year 700. Li Po (699–762) seems an effortless singer, so accomplished
is his language. He is a romantic, filled with *joie de vivre.* The two short
poems[12] that represent him here can only hint at the range and variety of
his verse.

To Someone Far Away

When she was here
     pretty darling
          flowers filled the hall
Now she's gone
     pretty darling
          left her bed behind
On her bed
     th'embroidered coverlet
          rolled up
          never slept in again
Three years to the day
      still keeps
      the scent of her
Fragrance never lost
     pretty darling
     never came back
Yellow leaves falling
      when I think of her
white dew
     on green moss

On the Mountain: Question and Answer

You ask me:
     Why do I live
on this green mountain?
  I smile
  No answer
     My heart serene
On flowing water
      peachblow
      quietly going
      far away
This is another earth
      another sky
No likeness
     to that human world below

Tu Fu (712–770) is often considered the greatest of Chinese poets and the most difficult to translate. His verse is so condensed, flawless in its formal patterns, full of feeling—subtle, compassionate, tragic. He lived in the brilliant age of the Emperor Ming Huang, and then after a terrible rebellion in 756, he survived civil war, prison, and exile. Those who are unfamiliar with Chinese poetry may tend to imagine it as a kind of *Chinoiserie,* all willow trees and little bridges. On the contrary there are strong poems of social protest and moving poems about the sorrows of war. In "A Song of War Chariots," Tu Fu describes the men sent off to guard the northwest frontier, a recurring source of anguish in Chinese history.

A Song of War Chariots

The war-chariots rattle,
The war-horses whinny.
Each man of you has a bow and a quiver at his belt.
Father, mother, son, wife, stare at you going,
Till dust shall have buried the bridge beyond Ch'ang-an.
And the sound of their sorrow goes up to the clouds;
And every time a bystander asks you a question,
You can only say to him that you have to go.
. . . We remember others at fifteen sent north to guard the river
And at forty sent west to cultivate the camp-farms.
The mayor wound their turbans for them when they started out.
With their turbaned hair white now, they are still at the border,
At the border where the blood of men spills like the sea—
And still the heart of Emperor Wu is beating for war.
. . . Do you know that, east of China's mountains, in two hundred
  districts
And in thousands of villages, nothing grows but weeds,
And though strong women have bent to the ploughing,
East and west the furrows all are broken down?
. . . Men of China are able to face the stiffest battle,
But their officers drive them like chickens and dogs.
Whatever is asked of them,
Dare they complain?
For example, this winter
Held west of the gate,
Challenged for taxes,
How could they pay?
. . . We have learned that to have a son is bad luck—
It is very much better to have a daughter
Who can marry and live in the house of a neighbour,
While under the sod we bury our boys.
. . . Go to the Blue Sea, look along the shore
At all the old white bones forsaken—
New ghosts are wailing there now with the old,
Loudest in the dark sky of a stormy day.[13]

Far up the River

A pair of golden orioles
Sings in the bright green willows.
A line of white egrets crosses
The clear blue sky. The window
Frames the western mountains, white
With the snows of a thousand years.
Anchored to the pilings are
Boats from eastern Wu,
Three thousand miles from home.[14]

Thoughts on a Night Journey

Reeds by the bank bending, stirred by the breeze,
High-masted boat advancing alone in the night,
Stars drawn low by the vastness of the plain,
The moon rushing forward in the river's flow.
How should I look for fame to what I have written?
In age and sickness, how continue to serve?
Wandering, drifting, what can I take for likeness?
—A gull that wheels alone between earth and sky.[15]

In 1969, in an oasis of the Central Asian desert, a poem was found that had been copied out in the year 820, by a Uigur named Kanmaur.[16] It was a poem of social protest, "The Charcoal Seller," by Po Chu-i, the best-loved and most famous poet of the generation after Li Po and Tu Fu. The poem had traveled two thousand miles westward from Ch'ang-an where Po Chu-i lived and wrote. He was the one Chinese poet known and endlessly quoted by the courtiers and ladies of Murasaki's long novel, *The Tale of Genji,* in those faraway islands of Japan to the eastward. Po Chu-i wrote what is practically a complete autobiography in verse. Already quoted in chapter 1 is his poem, "Alarm at First Entering the Yangtze Gorges."

Madly Singing in the Mountains

There is no one among men that has not a special failing:
And my failing consists in writing verses.
I have broken away from the thousand ties of life:
But this infirmity still remains behind.
Each time that I look at a fine landscape:
Each time that I meet a loved friend,
I raise my voice and recite a stanza of poetry
And am glad as though a God had crossed my path.
Ever since the day I was banished to Hsün-yang
Half my time I have lived among the hills.

And often, when I have finished a new poem,
Alone I climb the road to the Eastern Rock.
I lean my body on the banks of white stone:
I pull down with my hands a green cassia branch.
My mad singing startles the valleys and hills:
The apes and birds all come to peep.
Fearing to become a laughing-stock to the world,
I choose a place that is unfrequented by men.[17]

The Red Cockatoo

Sent as a present from Annam—
A red cockatoo.
Coloured like the peach-tree blossom,
Speaking with the speech of men.
And they did to it what is always done
To the learned and eloquent.
They took a cage with stout bars
And shut it up inside.[18]

Here is the beginning of a long poem by Po Chu-i. You may like to compare his description with Li Ch'eng's painting reproduced on page 50. The poet would, however, have been familiar with the landscape painting of his own earlier time, "the blue and green style," paintings in color, and not in the monochrome ink of Li Ch'eng's painting.

The Temple

Autumn: the ninth year of Yuan-ho;
The eighth month, and the moon swelling her arc.
It was then I travelled to the Temple of Wu-chen,
A temple terraced on Wang Shun's Hill.
While still the mountain was many leagues away,
Of scurrying waters we heard the plash and fret.
From here the traveller, leaving carriage and horse,
Begins to wade through the shallows of the Blue Stream,
His hand pillared on a green holly-staff,
His feet treading the torrent's white stones.
A strange quiet stole on ears and eyes,
That knew no longer the blare of the human world.
From mountain-foot gazing at mountain-top,
Now we doubted if indeed it could be climbed;
Who had guessed that a path deep hidden there
Twisting and bending crept to the topmost brow?

*   *   *

I turned away, and saw the Temple gate—
Scarlet eaves flanked by steeps of green;
'Twas as though a hand had ripped the mountain-side
And filled the cleft with a temple's walls and towers.
Within the gate, no level ground;
Little ground, but much empty sky.
Cells and cloisters, terraces and spires
High and low, followed the jut of the hill.
On rocky plateaux with no earth to hold
Were trees and shrubs, gnarled and very lean.
Roots and stems stretched to grip the stone;
Humped and bent, they writhed like a coiling snake.
In broken ranks pine and cassia stood,
Through the four seasons forever shady-green.
On tender twigs and delicate branches breathing
A quiet music played like strings in the wind.
Never pierced by the light of sun or moon,
Green locked with green, shade clasping shade.
A hidden bird sometimes softly sings;
Like a cricket's chirp sounds its muffled song.[19]

In an enchanting eighteenth-century painting, *Conversation in Autumn*, by Hua Yen (1682–c. 1762) in ink and delicate color, two scholars are discussing a famous "prose poem" written by Ou-yang Hsiu (1007–1072) in the Sung dynasty.

The Sound of Autumn

One night when I was reading I heard a sound coming from the southwest. I listened in alarm and said:

"Strange! At first it was a patter of drops, a rustle in the air; all at once it is hooves stampeding, breakers on a shore; it is as though huge waves were rising startled in the night, in a sudden downpour of wind and rain. When it collides with something, it clatters and clangs, gold and iron ring together; and then it is as though soldiers were advancing against an enemy, running swiftly with the gag between their teeth, and you hear no voiced command, only the tramping of men and horses."

I said to the boy, "What is this sound? Go out and look."

The boy returned and told me:

"The moon and stars gleam white and pure, the bright river is in the sky, nowhere is there any sound of man; the sound is over among the trees."

"Alas, how sad!" I answered. "This is the sound of autumn, why has it come? If you wish to know the signs which distinguish autumn, its colours are pale and mournful, mists dissolve and the clouds are gathered away; its face is clear and bright, with the sky high overhead

Hua Yen
Conversation in Autumn (detail)

Hua Yen
Conversation in Autumn

and a sun of crystal; its breath is harsh and raw, and pierces our flesh and bones; its mood is dreary and dismal, and the mountains and rivers lie desolate. Therefore the sound which distinguishes it is keen and chill, and bursts out in shrieks and screams. The rich, close grass teems vivid green, the thriving verdure of splendid trees delights us; then autumn sweeps the grass and its colour changes, touches the trees and their leaves drop. The power by which it lays waste and scatters far and wide is the unexpended fury of the breath of heaven and earth."[20]

Only about half of the passage is quoted here, but it reminds us of the sensitivity to the changing seasons that underlies so much of Chinese and Japanese poetry.

Something of the charm of the poet, painter, and statesman, Su Tung-p'o (1037–1101), who was a follower and friend of Ou-yang Hsiu, is conveyed in this little poem written in tribute after his death.

> When with tall hat and firm baton he stood in council,
> The crowds were awed at the dignity of the statesman in him.
> But when in cloth cap he strolled with cane and sandals,
> He greeted little children with gentle smiles.[21]

A poem and two prose poems by Su Tung-p'o about the Red Cliff in the gorges of the Yangtze (where a famous naval battle had been fought in ancient times) provided the subject for many Chinese paintings in an extraordinary variety of compositions. Nothing could be more graphic than the album leaf in fan shape reproduced here, although no photograph can do justice to the swirling water around the little boat, "shallow as a leaf," in which the poet and his two friends are being paddled close under the Red Cliff.

Li Sung *The Red Cliff*

The Red Cliff, I

In the autumn of the year *jen-hsu* (1082), on the sixteenth day of the seventh month, I took some guests on an excursion by boat under the Red Cliff. A cool wind blew gently, without starting a ripple. I raised my cup to pledge the guests; and we chanted the Full Moon ode, and sang out the verse about the modest lady. After a while the moon came up above the hills to the east, and wandered between the Dipper and the Herdboy Star; a dewy whiteness spanned the river, merging the light on the water into the sky. We let the tiny reed drift on its course, over ten thousand acres of dissolving surface which streamed to the horizon, as though we were leaning on the void with the winds for chariot, on a journey none knew where, hovering above as though we had left the world of men behind us and risen as immortals on newly sprouted wings.

Soon, when the wines we drank had made us merry, we sang this verse tapping the gunwales:

> Cinnamon oars in front, magnolia oars behind
> Beat the transparent brightness, thrust upstream against flooding
>   light.
> So far, the one I yearn for,
> The girl up there at the other end of the sky!

One of the guests accompanied the song on a flute. The notes were like sobs, as though he were complaining, longing, weeping, accusing; the wavering resonance lingered, a thread of sound which did not snap off, till the dragons underwater danced in the black depths, and a widow wept in our lonely boat.

I solemnly straightened my lapels, sat up stiffly, and asked the guest: "Why do you play like this?"

The guest answered:

> "'Full moon, stars few
> Rooks and magpies fly south . . .

"Was it not Ts'ao Ts'ao who wrote this verse? Gazing toward Hsia-k'ou in the west, Wu-ch'ang in the east, mountains and river winding around him, stifling in the close green . . . was it not here that Ts'ao Ts'ao was hemmed in by young Chou? At the time when he smote Ching-chou and came eastwards with the current down from Chiang-ling, his vessels were prow by stern for a thousand miles, his banners hid the sky; looking down on the river winecup in hand, composing his poem with lance slung crossways, truly he was the hero of his age, but where is he now? And what are you and I compared with him? Fishermen and woodcutters on the river's isles, with fish and shrimps and deer for mates, riding a boat as shallow as a leaf, pouring each other drinks from bottlegourds; mayflies visiting between heaven and earth, infinitesimal grains in the vast sea, mourning the passing of our instant of life, envying the long river which never ends! Let me cling to a flying immortal and roam far off, and live for ever with the full moon in my arms! But knowing that this art is not easily learned, I commit the fading echoes to the sad wind."

"Have you really understood the water and the moon?" I said. "The one streams past so swiftly yet is never gone; the other for ever waxes and wanes yet finally has never grown nor diminished. For if you look at the aspect which changes, heaven and earth cannot last for one blink; but if you look at the aspect which is changeless, the worlds within and outside you are both inexhaustible, and what reasons have you to envy anything?

"Moreover, each thing between heaven and earth has its owner, and even one hair which is not mine I can never make part of me. Only the cool wind on the river, or the full moon in the mountains, caught by the ear becomes a sound, or met by the eye changes to colour; no one forbids me to make it mine, no limit is set to the use of it; this is the inexhaustible treasury of the creator of things, and you and I can share in the joy of it."

The guest smiled, consoled. We washed the cups and poured more wine. After the nuts and savouries were finished, and the winecups and dishes lay scattered around, we leaned pillowed back to back in the middle of the boat, and did not notice when the sky turned white in the east.[22]

Another version of the Red Cliff theme appears in a beautiful hand scroll in the Freer Gallery by Shen Chou's friend and distinguished follower, Wen Cheng-ming. Painted about three hundred and fifty years after the Li Sung album leaf, the central motif—the poet, his two friends,

Wen Cheng-ming
The Red Cliff (detail)

the oarsman, and the boat—have changed very little. But the artist, like the writer in the opening quotation of this Literary Interlude, has known how to expand "the horizon to make space infinite."

Writing is in itself a joy,
Yet saints and sages have long since held it in awe.
For it is Being, created by tasking the Great Void,
And 'tis sound rung out of Profound Silence.
In a sheet of paper is contained the Infinite,
And, evolved from an inch-sized heart, an endless panorama.
The words, as they expand, become all-evocative,
The thought, still further pursued, will run the deeper,
Till flowers in full blossom exhale all-pervading fragrance,
And tender boughs, their saps running, grow to a whole jungle of
   splendor.
Bright winds spread luminous wings, quick breezes soar from the
   earth,
And, nimbus-like amidst all these, rises the glory of the literary
   world.[23]

T'ao Cheng *Chrysanthemums and Cabbages* (detail)

Li Shih-hsing *Old Trees by a Cool Spring* (detail)

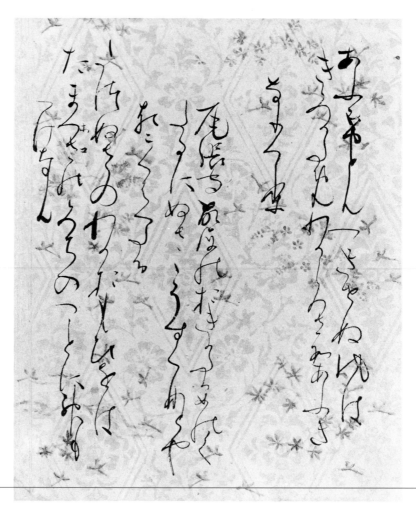

9

JAPAN

Page in "Grass Writing"
from the Collected Poems
of Ki-no Tsurayuki

The pleasantest of all diversions is to sit alone under the lamp, a book
spread out before you, and to make friends with people of a distant
past you have never known.[1]

Japanese poetry in translation began to be known in Europe in the
second half of the nineteenth century, at a time when Manet, Monet,
Degas, Toulouse-Lautrec, and others were making creative use of fresh
visual images borrowed from Japanese prints.

Although there were important translations of Japanese poetry being
made into English at that time, it was the poets who were young in the
first half of the twentieth century who were most deeply influenced by
Chinese and Japanese literature: William Butler Yeats, Ezra Pound, D. H.
Lawrence, and the Imagists—John Gould Fletcher and Amy Lowell,
among others. We are fortunate that many distinguished scholars and

poets have been translating and publishing Japanese works since the early years of this century, but in order to perceive the special rhythms and nuances of Japanese poetry, we would have to know the language itself.

What follows are examples of Japanese poetry, and of prose that is closely involved with poetry, in an effort to point out the extraordinary visual awareness of the Japanese people, and something of their response to Nature, their personal feelings. These quotations arrange themselves in three groups: first, lyrical poems from three of the early anthologies; second, brief selections from prose that is closely involved with poetry (in this group, Lady Murasaki's *The Tale of Genji* is the supreme example); and third, some writings that clearly show the influence of Zen Buddhism.

The oldest of the anthologies and the greatest is the *Manyoshu,* compiled in A.D. 760. Emperors, their consorts, noblemen, court ladies, and common folk are among those to whom the more than four thousand poems are attributed. A Japanese poem does not rhyme; the form depends on the number of syllables in a line and the number of lines. A form frequently used in the *Manyoshu* (although there are longer poems) is the *waka* composed of thirty-one syllables in lines of five, seven, five, followed by two seven-syllable lines.

The five poems that follow are translated from the *Manyoshu:*

Climbing Kagu-yama and Looking Upon the Land

Countless are the mountains in Yamato,
But perfect is the heavenly hill of Kagu;
When I climb it and survey my realm,
Over the wide plain the smoke-wreaths rise and rise,
Over the wide lake the gulls are on the wing;
A beautiful land it is, the Land of Yamato![2]   —Emperor Jomei

Addressed to a Young Woman

Over the river ferry of Saho,
Where the sanderlings cry—
When can I come to you,
Crossing on horseback
The crystal-clear shallows?[3] —Otomo Yakamochi

Do Not Smile to Yourself

Do not smile to yourself
Like a green mountain
With a cloud drifting across it.
People will know we are in love.[4] —Lady Otomo of Sakanoe

To a Lean Man

Iwamaro, I tell you,
Catch and eat eels!
They are good, they say,
For summer loss of flesh.

Yet, no matter how lean you are,
It is better to be alive.
So drown not yourself in the river
Trying to catch an eel![5]

—Otomo Yakamochi

Seeing a Dead Body Lying Among the Stones on the Island of Saminé in the Province of Sanuki

O Sanuki of beautiful seaweed
On which I never tire to look!
So fair is the province
Because of its origin,
And so hallowed the land
For its divinity—
With the very face of a god
Enduring full and perfect
With heaven and earth, with sun and moon.
I, travelling from place to place,
Embarked at Naka's haven
And thence sailed on,
When with the tide the wind arose,
Blowing from the dwelling-place of clouds.
I saw the billows racing on the sea,
And white surges beat upon the shore.
In fear of the whale-haunted sea
We rowed, straining the oars,
And sought, of all the islands thereabout,
Saminé, the island of renown,
And on its rugged coast
We built a hut for shelter.

There I found you, poor man!—
Outstretched on the beach,
On this rough bed of stones,
Amid the busy voices of the waves.

If I but knew where was your home,
I would go and tell;
If your wife but knew,
She would come to tend you.

She, knowing not even the way hither,
Must wait, must ever wait,
Restlessly hoping for your return—
Your dear wife—alas!

Envoys

Had your wife been with you,
She would have gathered food for you—
Starworts on Sami's hill-side—
But now is not their season past?

On the rugged beach
Where the waves come surging in from sea
You sleep, O luckless man,
Your head among the stones![6]

—Kakinomoto Hitomaro

A "Collection of Ancient and Modern Poems," the *Kokinshu,* was gathered together in 905 by order of the emperor. Here are three poems, three *waka.* One is by a famous woman poet, Ono no Komachi, whose story is movingly told in the No plays. Celebrated for her beauty, cruel to her lovers, she lived into a tragic old age.

They say there is
A still pool even in the middle of
The rushing whirlpool,—

Why is there none in the whirlpool of my love?[7]

—Anonymous

If only, when one heard
That Old Age was coming
One could bolt the door,

Answer "not at home"
And refuse to meet him![8]

—Anonymous

A thing which fades
With no outward sign—
Is the flower

Of the heart of man
In this world![9]

—Ono no Komachi

With three *waka* from the *Shinkokinshu,* or "New Collection of Ancient and Modern Poems," dated 1205, we conclude excerpts from the early anthologies. Melancholy in mood, the poems in this group are admired for their formal perfection.

先芸天皇後一品武

Artist Unknown
The Poet Taira-no-Kanemori

Hasegawa Tohaku
Pine Trees (detail)

The hanging raindrops
Have not dried from the needles
Of the fir forest
Before the evening mist
Of autumn rises.[10]

—The priest Jakuren

The irises,
Their petals damp, are fragrant.
Listen! The cuckoos
Are calling now, this rainy
Evening in May.[11]

—Fujiwara no Yoshitsune

In this wide landscape
I see no cherry blossoms
And no crimson leaves—
Evening in autumn over
A straw-thatched hut by the bay.[12]

—Fujiwara no Teika

Donald Keene observed that cherry blossoms and crimson leaves are conventional phrases used in describing spring and autumn. "In this wide landscape," it is almost as if we were looking at a monochrome ink painting.[13]

The *Ise Monogatari, The Tales of Ise* (pronounced Ee-say), is halfway between a collection of lyric poetry and a narrative or tale. A paragraph or two of prose sets the scene for each poem. The hero of the *Tales,* "a certain man," is thought to be Ariwara no Narihira (823–880), a nobleman famous in love and poetry. Episodes from the *Tales of Ise* have provided motifs for painters and designers ever since the tenth century. Scenarios of the sections quoted here and in chapter 15 appear again and again as paintings, screens, and fans, or as designs on lacquer boxes. The screen painting shown on page 144 is an eighteenth-century illustration of the pass through the mountains, "overgrown with ivy vines and maples."

On they journeyed to the province of Suruga. At Mount Utsu the road they were to follow was dark, narrow, and overgrown with ivy vines and maples. As they contemplated it with dismal forebodings, a wandering ascetic appeared and asked, "What are you doing on a road like this?" The man, recognizing him as someone he had once known by sight, gave him a message for a lady in the capital:

Suruga naru	Beside Mount Utsu
Utsu no yamabe no	In Suruga
Utsutsu ni mo	I can see you
Yume ni mo hito ni	Neither waking
Awanu narikeri.	Nor, alas, even in my dreams.

At Mount Fuji a pure white snow had fallen, even though it was the end of the Fifth Month.[14]

The greatest of the narrative tales and generally considered the masterpiece of Japanese literature is *The Tale of Genji* (the "g" is hard, as in get) by Lady Murasaki Shikibu. A lady-in-waiting to the empress, she was writing in the years just after A.D. 1000. The story of Genji, the Shining Prince, begins with the interplay of love and jealousy, of poetry and the arts, and moves toward an increasingly somber conclusion in which the Buddhist theme of the transiency of life hovers over the complex cast of characters like a long, gray cloud in a Japanese hand scroll.

Although a work of prose fiction, poetry moves through the story in two ways. Ladies and gentlemen of the court often carry on a conversation in impromptu verse or in quotations from the classic poetry of Japan and China. Letters exchanged between lovers were poems written in an elegant hand, and tied up with an appropriate blossom or branch of pine or willow. Some eight hundred poems are scattered through the text. But poetry is also represented in more subtle ways: in a scene echoed later with variations, in a situation almost duplicated in another generation. Poetry is interwoven in the structure of the novel itself, like the motifs of a musical composition. Here are two passages in which, against contrasting backgrounds—the Emperor's Palace and a lonely seacoast—the evening light illuminates the figure of Genji, the Shining Prince. The first is from a chapter called "Autumn Excursion."

> The royal excursion to the Suzaku Palace took place toward the middle of the Tenth Month. The emperor's ladies lamented that they would not be present at what was certain to be a most remarkable concert. Distressed especially at the thought that Fujitsubo should be deprived of the pleasure, the emperor ordered a full rehearsal at the main palace. Genji and Tō no Chūjō danced "Waves of the Blue Ocean." Tō no Chūjō was a handsome youth who carried himself well, but beside Genji he was like a nondescript mountain shrub beside a blossoming cherry. In the bright evening light the music echoed yet more grandly through the palace and the excitement grew; and though the dance was a familiar one, Genji scarcely seemed of this world. As he intoned the lyrics his auditors could have believed they were listening to the Kalavinka bird of paradise. The emperor brushed away tears of delight, and there were tears in the eyes of all the princes and high courtiers as well. As Genji rearranged his dress at the end of his song and the orchestra took up again, he seemed to shine with an ever brighter light.[15]

The second passage is from a chapter about Prince Genji's exile at Suma where he is living with a few companions in a rough little house by the sea, far from the capital and their loved ones. The time is again autumn.

There was a profusion of flowers in the garden. Genji came out, when the evening colors were at their best, to a gallery from which he had a good view of the coast. His men felt chills of apprehension as they watched him, for the loneliness of the setting made him seem like a visitor from another world. In a dark robe tied loosely over singlets of figured white and aster-colored trousers, he announced himself as "a disciple of the Buddha" and slowly intoned a sutra, and his men thought that they had never heard a finer voice. From offshore came the voices of fishermen raised in song. The barely visible boats were like little seafowl on an utterly lonely sea, and as he brushed away a tear induced by the splashing of oars and the calls of wild geese overhead, the white of his hand against the jet black of his rosary was enough to bring comfort to men who had left their families behind.[16]

The Tale of Genji has had enormous influence on the literature, the painting, and the decorative arts of Japan. Other aspects of the story will reappear in later chapters of this book.

A contemporary of Murasaki Shikibu, and like her, lady-in-waiting to an Empress, Sei Shonagon is celebrated for her *Pillow Book,* a kind of journal or collection of personal notes. She is witty, observant, opinionated, and delightful. Here are the opening and closing passages of *The Pillow Book* with a few brief excerpts in between.

In Spring It Is the Dawn

In spring it is the dawn that is most beautiful. As the light creeps over the hills, their outlines are dyed a faint red and wisps of purplish cloud trail over them.

In summer the nights. Not only when the moon shines, but on dark nights too, as the fireflies flit to and fro, and even when it rains, how beautiful it is!

In autumn the evenings, when the glittering sun sinks close to the edge of the hills and the crows fly back to their nests in threes and fours and twos; more charming still is a file of wild geese, like specks in the distant sky. When the sun has set, one's heart is moved by the sound of the wind and the hum of the insects.

In winter the early mornings. It is beautiful indeed when snow has fallen during the night, but splendid too when the ground is white with frost; or even when there is no snow or frost, but it is simply very cold and the attendants hurry from room to room stirring up the fires and bringing charcoal, how well this fits the season's mood! But as noon approaches and the cold wears off, no one bothers to keep the braziers alight, and soon nothing remains but piles of white ashes.[17]

A Preacher Ought to Be Good-Looking

A preacher ought to be good-looking. For, if we are properly to understand his worthy sentiments, we must keep our eyes on him while he speaks; should we look away, we may forget to listen. Accordingly an ugly preacher may well be the source of sin. . . . [18]

Splendid Things

Chinese brocade. A sword with a decorated scabbard. The grain of the wood in a Buddhist statue. Long flowering branches of beautifully coloured wistaria entwined about a pine tree. . . .
    Grape-coloured material.
    Anything purple is splendid, be it flowers, thread, or paper. Among purple flowers, however, I do not like the iris despite its gorgeous colour. What makes the costume of Sixth Rank Chamberlains so attractive when they are on night duty is the purple trousers.
    A large garden all covered with snow. [19]

It Is Getting So Dark

It is getting so dark that I can scarcely go on writing; and my brush is all worn out. Yet I should like to add a few things before I end.
    I wrote these notes at home, when I had a good deal of time to myself and thought no one would notice what I was doing. Everything that I have seen and felt is included. Since much of it might appear malicious and even harmful to other people, I was careful to keep my book hidden. But now it has become public, which is the last thing I expected.
    One day Lord Korechika, the Minister of the Centre, brought the Empress a bundle of notebooks. 'What shall we do with them?' Her Majesty asked me. 'The Emperor has already made arrangements for copying the "Records of the Historian".'
    'Let me make them into a pillow,' I said.
    'Very well,' said Her Majesty. 'You may have them.'
    I now had a vast quantity of paper at my disposal, and I set about filling the notebooks with odd facts, stories from the past, and all sorts of other things, often including the most trivial material. On the whole I concentrated on things and people that I found charming and splendid; my notes are also full of poems and observations on trees and plants, birds and insects. I was sure that when people saw my book they would say, 'It's even worse than I expected. Now one can really tell what she is like.' After all, it is written entirely for my own amusement and I put things down exactly as they came to me. How could my casual jottings possibly bear comparison with the many impressive books that exist in our time? Readers have declared,

At Muro-ji Photograph by the author

Island and the Sea Photograph by the author

Mountain View from Koyasan Photograph by the author

Japanese Girl at a Window Photograph by the author

Fisherman at Toba Photograph by the author

Fukae Roshu *The Ivy Lane*

however, that I can be proud of my work. This has surprised me greatly; yet I suppose it is not so strange that people should like it, for, as will be gathered from these notes of mine, I am the sort of person who approves of what others abhor and detests the things they like.

Whatever people may think of my book, I still regret that it ever came to light.[20]

Turning now to a third group of excerpts from Japanese literature—writings that show clearly the influence of Zen—one can hardly try to suggest in brief quotations the power and restraint of the aristocratic No drama of medieval Japan. But this passage about the secret arts of the actor by Seami Motokiyo (1363–1443), the greatest writer of No plays, tells us something of the concentration, the discipline, the experience, that are required even today of actors who perform plays of the traditional No theatre. The passage is deeply infused with the spirit of Zen.

Sometimes spectators of the *Nō* say that the moments of "no action" are the most enjoyable. This is one of the actor's secret arts. Dancing and singing, movements on the stage, and the different types of miming are all acts performed by the body. Moments of "no action" occur in between. When we examine why such moments without action are enjoyable, we find that it is due to the underlying spiritual strength of the actor which unremittingly holds the attention. He does

Scene from a No Play Photograph

not relax the tension when the dancing or singing comes to an end or at intervals between the dialogue and the different types of miming, but maintains an unwavering inner strength. This feeling of inner strength will faintly reveal itself and bring enjoyment. However, it is undesirable for the actor to permit this inner strength to become obvious to the audience. If it is obvious, it becomes an act, and is no longer "no action." The actions before and after an interval of "no action" must be linked by entering the state of mindlessness in which the actor conceals even from himself his own intent. The ability to move audiences depends, thus, on linking all the artistic powers with one mind.[21]

The same sense that more is implied than is stated may be found in the miniature art of haiku poetry. That small concise poem (seventeen syllables in Japanese) is probably more familiar to us than any other form in Japanese literature. Haiku came out of a verse form, a sort of happening called "linked verse." At its simplest, linked verse consisted of the *waka* of five lines, but composed by two poets, one writing the first three lines, the other composing the last two lines. This led to the cooperative enterprise of three or more poets writing whole sequences of stanzas, each linked to the previous one by some association of ideas. Haiku came into being as a new form, an independent poem made out of the opening unit of "free linked verse" just three lines of five, seven, five syllables, making a total of seventeen in all.

The poet Matsuo Basho (1644–1694) was chiefly responsible for finding fresh ways to compose linked verse, and to make out of the concise haiku the "distillation of a great poet's thought."[22] One of his early haiku is also one of the most famous:

> The ancient pond
> A frog leaps in
> The sound of the water.[23]

Donald Keene observes that in the first line Basho gives us the eternal component of the poem, the timeless, motionless waters of the pond. The second line gives us the momentary, represented by the movement of the frog. Their intersection is the sound of the water splashing. So it is the perception of a truth—the intersection of the timeless with time—that is the subject of the poem.

Here are three more haiku of Basho:

> On the withered branch
> A crow has alighted—
> Nightfall in autumn.[24]

> How rough a sea!
> and, stretching over Sado Isle,
> the Galaxy. . . . [25]

The sea darkens,
The cries of the seagulls
Are faintly white.[26]

Toward the end of his life, Basho set out on a journey to visit places famous in poetry and history, and to deepen his own spirit. *The Narrow Road to the Deep North* is the last of his five journals or travel diaries interspersed with poems. A slim paperback in Penguin Classics, it is a book to treasure. Here are the opening paragraphs, and part of Basho's account of a visit to the islands of Matsushima.

Days and months are travellers of eternity. So are the years that pass by. Those who steer a boat across the sea, or drive a horse over the earth till they succumb to the weight of years, spend every minute of their lives travelling. There are a great number of ancients, too, who died on the road. I myself have been tempted for a long time by the cloud-moving wind—filled with a strong desire to wander. . . .

It was only towards the end of last autumn that I returned and they all came with me on the boat to keep me company for the first few miles. When we got off the boat at Senju, however, the thought of the three thousand miles before me suddenly filled my heart, and neither the houses of the town nor the faces of my friends could be seen by my tearful eyes except as a vision.

Yosa Buson
Basho's Departure
(detail)

The passing spring,
Birds mourn,
Fishes weep
With tearful eyes.[27]

*   *   *

The islands are situated in a bay about three miles wide in every direction and open to the sea through a narrow mouth on the south-east side. Just as the River Sekkō in China is made full at each swell of the tide, so is this bay filled with the brimming water of the ocean, and innumerable islands are scattered over it from one end to the other. Tall islands point to the sky and level ones prostrate themselves before the surges of water. Islands are piled above islands, and islands are joined to islands, so that they look exactly like parents caressing their children or walking with them arm in arm. The pines are of the freshest green, and their branches are curved in exquisite lines, bent by the wind constantly blowing through them. Indeed, the beauty of the entire scene can only be compared to the most divinely endowed of feminine countenances, for who else could have created such beauty but the great god of nature himself? My pen strove in vain to equal this superb creation of divine artifice.[28]

For another vision of the islands of Matsushima you can turn to the screens by the painter Tawaraya Sotatsu on pages 214 and 215 and to a detail of those screens on page 218. In his own lifetime, Basho was regarded as a master, loved and honored by hundreds of pupils and followers.

The greatest writer of haiku verse in the next century was Yosa Buson (1716–1784). He revered Basho and even followed in his footsteps on his own journey to the north. Equally distinguished as a poet and a

Miyako, 1965 Photograph by Henri Cartier-Bresson

Ando Hiroshige
Morning Mist at Mishima

painter, here are three haiku by Buson with their compelling visual images. The first poem reminds us of a Japanese wood-block print.

> Blossoms on the pear—
>   and a woman in the moonlight
>   reads a letter there.[29]

> On the temple bell
>   has settled, and is fast asleep,
>   a butterfly.[30]

> Morning haze:
>   as in a painting of a dream,
>   men go their ways.[31]

D. T. Suzuki, the chief interpreter of Zen to the West, has observed that haiku embodies the spirit of Basho, its modern founder, and that the spirit of Basho is the spirit of Zen expressing itself in the seventeen syllables.[32] After reading the chapter "Zen, Sesshu, and the Way of Tea," you may want to return to these poems. The best haiku deserve reading more than once.

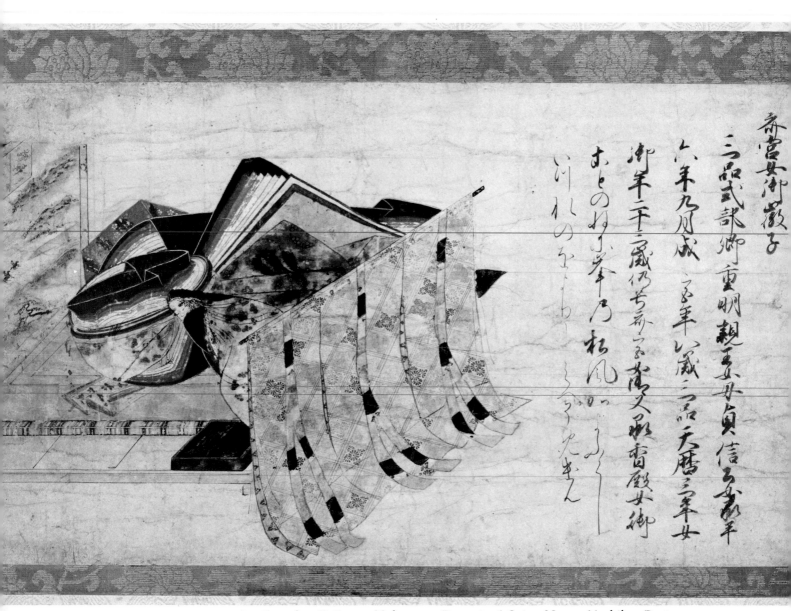

Attributed to Fujiwara Nobuzane *Portrait of Saigu Nyogo Yoshiko, Poetess*

An Invitation to the Arts of Japan

Mist at Nara Photograph by the author

10

THE ISLANDS, THE VEGETATION, THE SEAS

On the train to Kyoto,

August 13, 1932

Today the country is fresh and beautiful after yesterday's storm. It looks just like the prints come to life, even to the solitary fisherman or farmer going along in the middle distance. I am not sure whether I am in a Japanese rock garden in a dish, on a scenic railway, or in a wood-block print. But it is all continuously green and delightful, often within sight of the sea, and no ugly towns or factories at all.

153

These words turned up in a box of letters I had written on a long ago visit to the Far East. Whoever makes the trip now in the famous bullet train, traveling at a rate of 120 miles an hour, may still catch glimpses of extraordinary beauty along that coastal route. But power lines, factories, and housing projects will also be part of the landscape.

Nowadays, approaching Tokyo by air from Hawaii, you may find yourself flying over a cultivated landscape, intricate as a dish garden, before swooping down at Haneda Airport. Whatever the first glimpse, and in spite of industrialization, it is always the extraordinary variety of nature that impresses the visitor to Japan—mountains and narrow valleys, jutting capes and curving beaches, rice paddies and tea plantations, forests, waterfalls and swift rivers; a homeland that has always been reflected in the poetry, the paintings, and the gardens of Japan. It is a landscape often softened by mist and sometimes deluged with sudden, diagonal rain.

Lying off the great land mass of Asia in a chain stretching some thirteen hundred miles, Japan is made up of four main islands and of thousands of smaller islands and islets. Hokkaido in the north was made familiar to us in the West as a land of snow through television reporting of the Winter Olympics. In Honshu, largest of the four islands, lies the

Kansai Photograph

Ando Hiroshige
Shono (White Rain)

ancient heartland, the Yamato area, near Osaka and the seat of the early capitals—Nara, and then for many centuries, Kyoto. In 1185, powerful military rulers, the Shoguns, shifted the political capital to Kamakura, near modern Tokyo, on the Pacific shore, leaving the emperor and his court behind in Kyoto to continue their stylized existence. Finally, in 1615, the political capital was moved to Edo, later renamed Tokyo, or "Eastern Capital." Within sight of that pulsing city on any clear day rises Fujiyama to a height of 12,388 feet, a perfect cone, a symbol, and a presence.

Three islands—Honshu, the largest; Shikoku, richly cultivated; and Kyushu with its volcanoes and hot springs—enclose what the Japanese call "the Sea within Channels." Known to us as the Inland Sea, it is famous for its shrines and temples, its numerous wooded islands. In the mind of this writer, the Inland Sea will always remain a dream seen in brilliant moonlight as our ship made its way through channels, among islands, all the night long, slipping at last through the narrow straits of

The Inland Sea at Night Photograph

Shimonoseki just before dawn. Early lights in fishermen's houses climbed the steep, dark hillside against a thin wash of gray sky. Ahead lay the East China Sea and Shanghai.

In the poems translated from the early anthologies, you have already encountered the Japanese feeling for their land, for the "whale-haunted sea," the flowers and blossoming trees of spring, "the leafy treetops of summer mountains," the crickets and grasses of autumn. Characteristics of the four seasons are clearly distinguished. Nature, poetry, and the visual arts are all interwoven.

> The colored leaves
> Float like brocade
> On the River Tatsuta.[1]

And if an air of melancholy drifts like a mist across much of Japanese literature, we must remember the earthquakes and volcanoes, the typhoons and tidal waves, the perils of travel by land and by sea. Brevity of life was a stern reality, which made belief in the beneficence of nature all the more remarkable. In the early animism, the nature worship called Shinto, it was believed that *kami,* spirits or presences, inhabited rocks and trees, crops and animals, the cooking pot and the fire. The *kami* were everywhere. The spirits of ancestors were *kami,* to be treated with

Ise Shrine, View of Roofs over Fence Photograph

reverence. It was not so much that the *kami* needed to be appeased, but that appreciation and gratitude were due them. These simple beliefs of Shinto later became intertwined with the idea of the imperial family as a symbol of the nation, and even with ideas borrowed from Buddhism, when that new religion came in all its complexity from China by way of Korea.

This sense of gratitude for the beauty and kindliness of nature is nowhere more movingly expressed, even to the uninitiated traveler, than in the great Shinto shrines at Ise (pronounced Ee-say). Set in an ancient forest, the smaller shrine, the Geku, dedicated to the Cereal-Providing Goddess, is first encountered. About four miles beyond is the Naiku, dedicated to Amaterasu, the "Heaven-Great-Shining," Goddess of the Sun, ancestress of the imperial family. After crossing a wide-arching wooden bridge on foot, visitors pause for ritual purification by rinsing their hands and their mouths in the swift-running water of the Isuzu River. A long walk over clean gravel, under the towering cryptomeria trees, brings visitors to a flight of stone steps flanked by ancient tree trunks and rock outcroppings. Ascending to the level of the shrine buildings, one is faced by the closed wooden doors of a high surrounding fence. As an American architect who made this pilgrimage once observed, "The Ise Shrine is the most beautiful building I have never seen."

Aerial View of Ise, Inner Shrine Photograph

Only the priests attached to the Shrine, or a high priestess who was traditionally an emperor's daughter, and other members of the imperial family may enter the sacred precincts. Before the closed doors of the high enclosing fences, the pilgrim pauses, claps his hands, and offers a brief prayer. Most Japanese visitors look refreshed and pleased as they turn to descend the steps.

The shrine itself was never a gathering place for worshipers like a cathedral in the West. It was set apart as a dwelling place for a sacred spirit, and there her mirror—one of the three symbols of the imperial family—has always been kept. Although Ise has been the site of this shrine, according to ancient records, since at least the fourth century, the building itself has never been more than twenty years old. It is therefore always fresh, clean, and fragrant, a fit abiding place for the Goddess of the Sun. The last reconstruction was in 1973. Everything—even to the felling of the trees for posts and the thatching of the roof—is done as traditionally prescribed. The shrine will be rebuilt again in 1993 on an alternate adjoining site, now prepared and ready, covered with small

The Approach to the Naiku Shrine at Ise Photograph

round stones. The architect, Kenzo Tange, has observed that the ceremonial rebuilding of the Ise Shrine every twenty years is like adding an annual ring to the tree of Japanese tradition.

The Shrine of the Sun Goddess, with its subdued and subtle surfaces of natural wood and thatch, is surrounded by the deep shadows of a great forest. Half across the world, on top of the Acropolis at Athens stands the Parthenon, dedicated to Pallas Athena, goddess of wisdom, in the lucid air of Greece. The creamy marble columns have been washed over by the sun and sea winds for almost twenty-five centuries. It would take a wiser mind than mine to make something of this comparison. But the experience of either shrine is unforgettable, whether we respond to the site, the architecture, or to the expression of religious intuition.

The Ise Shrines are close to the Bay of Ise, which opens out to the Pacific and is known for its strange rock formations and small steep islands. The two other Shinto shrines with the longest tradition are also on the coast: at Sumiyoshi, at the head of the Inland Sea; and at Izumo, on the Sea of Japan, facing toward Korea. These seas are the home of whales and dolphins, of salmon and tuna and mackerel, of crabs and scallops and shrimps and oysters and the seaweeds—the sea that is never farther away than about eighty-five miles from any place in Japan.

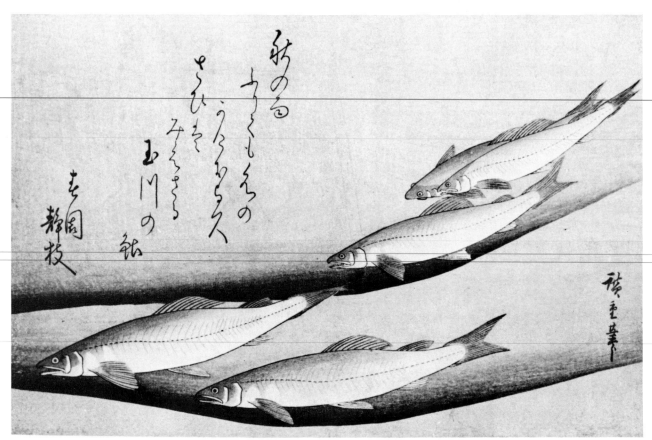

Ando Hiroshige *River Trout*

Deep Pot
Middle Jomon period

11
THE INHERITANCE FROM CHINA

Even our maps seem to emphasize the Pacific shores of Japan, with the focus on Tokyo and Fujiyama. We are less familiar with the coastline that faces the continent of Asia. The western shores of Honshu look across to Korea. The southern island of Kyushu faces northwest toward Korea, southwest toward China, while far away beyond the horizon lie the South Seas. Historians are much interested in how the earliest people came to Japan: some probably from the north when there were still land bridges from the mainland; others from South China, perhaps even from the South Seas.

The first people of the islands who have left objects to delight the eye made a vigorous pottery which dates from the Paleolithic or old Stone

Age, possibly as early as 6000 B.C. By 3000 or 2500 B.C., in the Neolithic, or new Stone Age, their coil-built pots and figurines were made in high relief with lively projections and continued to be impressed with the cord patterns that gave their name, Jomon (cord pattern), to the whole period lasting down to about 200 B.C. Expressive and often wildly exuberant, the pots made by the Jomon people appeal to the taste of our time in their verve and restless energy.

By the third century B.C., new waves of immigrants had brought wet-rice cultivation and the use of iron tools. A more settled life was developing and a quieter, more advanced sort of pottery made. This is known as the Yayoi culture, named for a site in Tokyo where the first pottery of this type was identified. The most highly organized center of population came to be the plain at the head of the Inland Sea, in the area of Osaka, Nara, and Kyoto today—the Yamato region. Due to Shinto beliefs about death and purification, the court moved to a new location after the death of each emperor, so there was no fixed capital. That this fishing, hunting, and rice-growing people were capable of large undertakings we know from numerous grave mounds dating from the third to the sixth centuries A.D. The tomb of the Emperor Nintoku (dated about A.D. 400), shaped like a keyhole and surrounded by moats, covers almost eighty acres not far from Osaka.

Terra-cotta sculpture based on hollow cylindrical forms with an engaging, sometimes haunting quality was made from about A.D. 200 to the coming of Buddhism. Known as *haniwa* (*hani* means clay, *wa* means circle), these unglazed, red-clay warriors, houses, horses, and other animals were not placed within the tomb like the grave figures of China but were set into the ground outside, in a circle to serve as guardians and to keep the grave mounds from washing away. So, long before the first great wave of Chinese influence, the Japanese had proved themselves intuitive craftsmen with skillful hands and sensitivity to materials—in this case to the possibilities of the pliant clay, rolled, impressed, modeled, pierced, or sliced. It has been said that it was the merging of these two cultures, the Jomon and the Yayoi, that produced the Japanese people.

The year 552 is considered the first significant contact of the court with Chinese Buddhism. The king of the Korean kingdom of Paikche sent a bronze image of the Buddha, some *sutras* (or scriptures) along with other gifts, and a letter praising the faith that had come all the way from India. He also asked for help from the Japanese court against his enemies in Korea.

Both political and religious reasons made the future of this foreign religion uncertain in Japan—anxiety that the worship of foreign gods might bring down the wrath of their native Shinto deities, and that foreign influences might undermine the power of certain noble families. It has been suggested that Buddhism established itself so much more quickly in Japan than in China because it did not have to contend with a

Haniwa Warrior
Sixth century

long-established culture or with Confucianism and Taoism. The native Japanese Shinto was a less complex, a more accommodating kind of faith. By the year 593, when the Empress Suiko made Prince Shotoku (572–622) her regent, Buddhism was securely established.

Shotoku-Taishi, as he is generally known, must have been a remarkable man. He studied the Buddhist scriptures; he ordered the construction of monasteries and temples; he dispatched students to China; he concerned himself with Confucian ideas and the arts of government. He was loved as a wise and prudent ruler. With Buddhism came the whole culture of China, including the possibility of a written language, which had not yet been devised in Japan. Architecture, city planning, sculpture, painting, poetry, music, costume, and the arts of government came with Buddhism from China. In the words of Sir George Sansom:

> It was as if a great magic bird flying on strong pinions across the ocean had brought to Japan all the elements of a new life—a new morality, the arts and crafts, and subtle metaphysics which had no counterpart in the native tradition.[1]

Craftsmen, musicians, and priests also came from Korea where considerable Chinese influence had already been absorbed. They found gifted and eager pupils in the Japanese.

We have spoken of the beauty and simplicity of the great Shinto shrine at Ise, a dwelling place for the spirit of the Sun Goddess, the imperial ancestress, who required no images as aids to worship. Let us look now at Horyu-ji, near Nara, a Buddhist monastic complex established by Shotoku-Taishi, the oldest and most honored of the existing Buddhist temples in Japan. The visitor enters on foot through the Great South Gate, with a glance at the huge guardian figures on either side. After passing through a second gate, he steps into the sand-colored courtyard, or cloister. Before him to the right is the Golden Hall, the Kondo, with its double roof. To the left stands the five-storied pagoda, its eaves fluted like the underside of a mushroom. Long covered verandas enclose three sides of the cloister. A lecture hall forms the far side opposite the gate. Ancient pines rising from the well-raked gravel connect the buildings with the world of Nature and with the gently wooded slopes beyond the enclosure. Said to be the oldest group of wooden buildings in the world, they were built without nails—beams fitted into beams like the old interlocking wooden puzzles children used to fit together into a cube. One has a sense of peace here, and of being on intimate terms with a long tradition.

Stone and bronze were readily available for making Buddhist images in China, but not in Japan. The Japanese had to master the arts of building, of casting in bronze, and of carving figures in wood from their

Aerial View of Horyu-ji
Near Nara Photograph

Tori Busshi *Shaka Triad*

plentiful forests. The gilt-bronze *Shaka Triad* on the high altar of the Golden Hall at Horyu-ji was completed in 623 and signed by the sculptor, Tori Busshi, in an inscription that dedicates the image to the salvation of Prince Shotoku, who had recently died. Shaka, the historical Buddha, sits in the position of meditation wearing a monk's robe that falls in formal, rhythmic folds. His right hand is raised in the gesture of reassurance. His left hand is in the gift-bestowing gesture. On either side stand smaller Bodhisattvas wearing crowns and dressed in princely costumes with flaring draperies. This nearly symmetrical group on its pedestal was meant to be seen by the worshiper from a frontal position and from below. In spite of an apparent awkwardness in proportions, the sculptor's serious purpose comes through to us. Made in a time of great religious fervor in court circles, of eager temple-building, the Shaka image gives form to the presence of the divine.

Tori's father was a statue maker. His grandfather, also a sculptor, had come from China, bringing with him the tradition of contemporary Chinese sculpture of the sixth century. Tori's own style grew out of his family traditions and out of contact with more recent Buddhist images from Korea. Something of what the *Shaka Triad* inherited from China may be seen by comparing it to the large limestone Bodhisattva (c. 530) on page 34 with its frontal position, its "waterfall" draperies, the long stoles looped around the neck, the downcast almond-shaped eyes.

Quite different in feeling from the *Shaka Triad,* although of the same period, is this important small bronze *Miroku Bosatsu* (the Buddha-to-Be, or Bodhisattva Maitreya). Gentleness and grace, inner serenity and outward calm, are combined in this appealing figure.

Suiko period (Japan)
Miroku Bosatsu
(see also page 178)

The *Shaka Triad* is just one among many famous early Buddhist images preserved at Horyu-ji and in the great temples of nearby Nara. The Japanese know how to preserve their treasures and to study them in detail. As a result of this respect for the past, sculpture in bronze and architecture in wood of the seventh and eighth centuries survive to this day in Japan although their counterparts in China have long since been destroyed by Buddhist persecutions and civil war.

An unfortunate exception to preservation in Japan are the murals on the four walls of the Golden Hall at Horyu-ji, destroyed by an accidental fire in 1949. The building itself was also damaged but has now been carefully restored. Copies of the paintings in their original size can be seen in Tokyo at the National Museum. They had been photographed in detail. But this was an immense loss, since no comparable figure paintings have survived from the great Chinese temples of the T'ang period. The wall paintings are dated somewhere between 680 and 710. From the detail on page 166 showing the head of a Bodhisattva who stands on the Buddha's left, one can imagine how imposing these paintings must have been with their sure brushwork and effective color.

For the wealthiest and most influential of temples, Todai-ji, "the

Head of Bodhisattva
from the Golden Hall,
Horyu-ji (detail)

The Great Buddha (Daibutsu) from Todai-ji, Nara

Eastern Great Monastery," a colossal seated bronze Buddha was completed after many technical difficulties and dedicated in 753, almost exactly two hundred years after the arrival of the first bronze image from Korea. The Japanese craftsmen and builders now felt equal to any challenge. Fifty-three feet in height, covered with gold leaf from newly discovered mines in a distant province, the dedication ceremony in the Great Buddha Hall was attended by the whole court, all the princes, princesses, nobles, and dignitaries.

Just as the religious treasures have been preserved in the temples and monasteries of the Nara region, the secular treasures of the mid-eighth century have also been preserved in a storehouse called the Shoso-in. This storehouse of the Todai-ji is in reality a great log cabin on high massive piles. It contains about ten thousand objects of eighth-century art, among them the personal possessions, costumes, household goods of the Emperor Shomu, who died shortly after the ceremony of dedication. Presented to the temple by his widow, with some later additions, the treasure consisted of costumes, musical instruments, textiles of intricate weave—many of Near Eastern design—vessels of gold and silver, painted screens, examples of calligraphy, precious medicines, and much more. A kind of natural air-conditioning allowed the logs to dry out in late summer

Shoso-in Nara, Photograph

Five-string Biwa from the Shoso-in

to permit the circulation of air, and to swell in winter in order to keep out dampness. Many of the objects are Chinese from the T'ang capital at the height of its glory; others are from Iran, from India and Central Asia. (The Shoso-in has traditionally been opened only once a year for cleaning and care, and for inspection by a very few selected scholars. Certain objects are exhibited from time to time at the National Museum in Tokyo.)

Once in the strange gray-green light of a typhoon that was sweeping through Nara, I stood—with the required official escort—right underneath the storehouse itself. As the rain came down in sheets, I thought with amazement that this wooden building had withstood the extravagances of nature and the passions of men for more than twelve hundred years. If we should imagine that the court robes and musical instruments, the ritual vessels and banners, from the coronation of Charlemagne (A.D. 800) and all his personal possessions had somehow been preserved, that would also be an extraordinary collection. But the level of sophistication and craftsmanship at that time in Europe was in no way comparable to the brilliant international style of eighth-century Buddhist art.

12
THE TASTE OF THE COURT
IN THE HEIAN PERIOD (794-1185)

The focus in the last chapter was on the impact of Chinese culture in Japan, and the gradual assimilation of that culture by the end of the eighth century. For the next four hundred years, the aristocracy, the educated elite, were involved in developing a highly individual, very Japanese culture, borrowing many elements from China, but with a style in the visual arts and literature, and a life style, that was distinctively their own.

In 794, apparently to get away from the powerful monasteries of Nara, the capital was moved to Heian-Kyo (later renamed Kyoto), where the imperial capital remained until 1868. This new and agreeable site

Nikko, the Sun Bodhisattva

Standing Kannon

surrounded by gentle hills was only twenty-six miles from Nara, but that was still a considerable distance by oxcart.

Since the Buddhist establishment had proved to be a great patron of the arts, new directions in the thought and teaching of what may be called the Buddhist church were bound to have an effect on the arts. In the first hundred years of the Heian period, however, sculpture still preserved qualities of the Chinese T'ang dynasty international style, as may be seen in *Nikko,* the Sun Bodhisattva with its fluid lines, its elegant drapery, and its quality of inner radiance.

Some tendencies developing in Heian sculpture may be seen in the contrast between two figures in the Museum of Fine Arts in Boston, the *Standing Kannon,* late eighth or early ninth century, and the *Miroku Bosatsu,* in wood, partially covered with gold lacquer, and made by a monk-sculptor, Kaikei, in 1189. It should be noted that Kaikei's sculpture is no longer made from a single block of wood, but by joining a number of pieces in a new technique known as *yosegi.* In three hundred years, the Bodhisattva image also has become more richly elegant, perhaps to our eyes has even become a fashionable figure. The taste of the court at the end of the Heian period has asserted itself, a court dominated by the Fujiwara family who married their daughters to emperors and kept the power in their own hands.

A similar sense of refinement can be felt in the Buddhist painting of Japan. These works provide an entirely different flavor from that of the monochrome ink paintings previously encountered in the art of China. Color in the scroll paintings is usually flat and decorative. There are delicate gold lines, smooth almost geometrical curves, and rich patterning, as you can see in the image called *Gohimitsu Bosatsu,* ("The Secret Five") on page 179. And the story of one Japanese priest who traveled to China just after the year 800 may be helpful in understanding how these strangely beautiful images reflect both the secular and religious life of Heian Japan.

Kukai (774–835), known after his death as Kobo Daishi, was one of the most brilliant and versatile figures of the Heian period. A priest, a painter, a sculptor, a poet, a saint, he is credited with having invented the Japanese script. He was concerned for education and was famous as a calligrapher, as well as a builder of roads. The sect of Buddhism that Kobo Daishi established was called *Shingon* (True Word). A sect of Esoteric Buddhism (*esoteric* means intended for or understood by only a few), it depended on Indian ideas that had recently been imported into China, on doctrines that he had absorbed from his Chinese teacher in the T'ang dynasty capital, Ch'ang-an (see page 33). It was Kobo Daishi who saw that the subtle and complex theology he brought back from China could be explained better through art than through words. "Eternal truth," he wrote, "transcends color, but only by means of color can it be understood. . . . Art is what reveals to us the state of perfection."[1] In this Kukai was like Suger (1081–1151), the abbot of St. Denis in France, who also felt strongly about the place of art in explaining and inspiring religious faith.

The complex of monasteries and temples that Kobo Daishi founded in 816 on Mount Koya was at a considerable distance from Kyoto. It still occupies a plateau on top of a splendidly forested mountain. Muro-ji, nearer to Nara, a temple that also has associations with Kobo Daishi, climbs up a steep, forested slope above a mountain stream. In these mountain temples, the Chinese tradition of a symmetrical temple plan followed at Nara gave way to the topography of a mountain site. This accommodation to nature, this tendency to asymmetry in architecture, as in the other arts, will remain a characteristic of the Japanese style.

Murasaki Shikibu (whose *The Tale of Genji* is quoted in "A Literary Interlude") and the court circles were mostly involved with another sect of Japanese Buddhism, the powerful Tendai. But there were no very fixed walls between Tendai, Shingon, and Jodo (Pure Land Buddhism), or even between Buddhism and Shinto. So when the luxury-loving people of the court began to tire of the ritual and gorgeous ceremonies of Shingon and Tendai, they welcomed a growing belief in Amida Buddha, the Lord of the Western Paradise. Faith in the promise of admission to his Paradise for all who simply repeated the formula, "I adore thee, O Buddha of Boundless Light," was a consolation to nobles and to illiterate peasants alike in a time of trouble, increasingly threatened by civil war.

Kaikei *Miroku Bosatsu*

Artist Unknown
Raigo: Descent of Amida

Phoenix Hall Byodo-in, Uji
Photograph

Around the year 1000, the greatest of the powerful Fujiwara family, Fujiwara no Michinaga, built a villa about ten miles south of Kyoto on the Uji River. In 1052, his son converted it into a temple, the Byodo-in, whose central feature, the Phoenix Hall, has been called the "chief surviving glory of Heian architecture."[2] Two phoenixes surmount the ridge pole of the central pavilion. The building itself is said to resemble a phoenix: the flanking pavilions being its outspread wings; another pavilion, the long tail stretched out behind. Reflected in the lotus pond, the pavilions are almost as enchanting to visitors today as they must have been to the "beautiful people" of the eleventh century. One can even imagine that Lady Murasaki herself may once have seen reflections of bright costumes in the water on some excursion to that new villa, the Byodo-in.

When the villa was turned into a temple, the sculptor Jocho was commissioned to create an image of Amida Buddha, of gilded wood, seated in meditation before a large and splendid halo, an image that fills the Phoenix Hall. On the walls around him are small carved angels descending to welcome, as in the Raigo painting, the souls of the dying. Painted scenes of landscape in the Western Paradise may still be dimly discerned on the walls. The interior of this hall, then, is a vision in three dimensions of Amida Buddha in his Western Paradise.

Jocho
Amida Buddha

What kind of people were the men and women in that circle of the great families around the emperor, families who supported the colorful ceremonies and splendid temples of Heian Buddhism, for whom poetry and music and painting were central in their cult of beauty? We can learn a great deal about them from the writings of the two women already quoted in "A Literary Interlude," Murasaki Shikibu and Sei Shonagon, who lived in the late tenth and early eleventh centuries. Men who were their contemporaries still wrote laws and chronicles, theology, and poetry in Chinese, a language that was used in much the same way as Latin was in medieval Europe. They even wrote their own language using Chinese characters. Women in Japanese court circles were not supposed to bother their heads with classical Chinese. But clever women of the upper class, lively, observant, and probably often bored with the role assigned to them in a highly artificial society, began to write down their own spoken language in the Japanese phonetic script called *hiragana.* One could hardly apply the word liberated to women in that hothouse society, yet for several generations the greatest literary talents in Japan were those of women.

In Sei Shonagon's *Pillow Book* a story is told approvingly by the empress about the education of an imperial concubine. The girl had been advised by her father to study calligraphy, to excel in music, and to memorize all the poems in the twenty volumes of the *Kokinshu* anthology. It appears then that education for young women was a training in aesthetic taste and skills. One can hardly imagine any society in which men and women have been more preoccupied with costume, with pattern and texture, and especially with the harmonies and contrasts of color, as these lines from *The Tale of Genji* tell us:

> For Murasaki he selected a lavender robe with a clear, clean pattern of rose-plum blossoms and a singlet of a fashionable lavender. For his little daughter there was a white robe lined with red and a singlet beaten to a fine glow. For the lady of the orange blossoms, a robe of azure with a pattern of seashells beautifully woven in quiet colors, and a crimson singlet, also fulled to a high sheen. For the new lady, a cloak of bright red and a robe of russet lined with yellow. Though pretending not to be much interested, Murasaki was wondering what sort of lady would go with these last garments.[3]

Or, in notes from Sei Shonagon about hunting costumes:

> Those that have been dyed a light orange color. White ones. Purple-red costumes whose outside and lining are of the same material. Costumes that are green outside and lined with purple. Those made of leaf-green, cherry-blossom, willow-green, or wistaria material. But for men's clothes any colour is all right.[4]

The following passage from *The Tale of Genji* illustrates how the art of calligraphy was involved with the religious life of Heian Japan, how the rule of taste and the talents of Prince Genji himself might, on occasion, be employed in copying out Buddhist scriptures.

> He had also made a copy of the Amitābha Sutra. Fearing that Chinese paper might begin to crumble after frequent use, he had ordered a fine, unmarked paper from the royal provisioner. He had been hard at work since spring and the results quite justified his labors. A glimpse of an unrolled corner was enough to tell the most casual observer that it was a masterpiece. The gilt lines were very good, but the sheen of

the black ink and the contrast with the paper were quite marvelous. I shall not attempt to describe the spindle, the cover, and the box, save to say that they were all of superb workmanship. On a new aloeswood stand with flared legs, it occupied a central place beside the holy trinity.[5]

In secular life, an elegant handwriting was important for success in politics, in love, and in poetry. In this passage, Prince Genji and his brother have been considering poems they had been writing on various kinds of paper.

> As the conversation ranged over the varieties of calligraphy and manuscripts, Genji brought out several books done in patchwork with old and new papers. The prince sent his son the chamberlain to bring some scrolls from his own library, among them a set of four on which the emperor Saga had copied selections from the *Manyoshu,* and a *Kokinshu* at the hand of the emperor Daigo, on azure Chinese papers with matching jade rollers, intricate damask covers of a darker blue, and flat Chinese cords in multicolored checkers. The writing was art of the highest order, infinitely varied but always gently elegant. Genji had a lamp brought near.
>
> "I could look at them for weeks and always see something new. Who in our own day can do more than imitate the smallest fragment?"[6]

The excerpts quoted from *The Tale of Genji,* both in this chapter and in "A Literary Interlude," have tried to suggest how poetry is interwoven into the fabric of the novel, how literary taste in court circles was cultivated by familiarity with Chinese and Japanese poetry and by the habit of composing verses on every sort of occasion. Sensibility in all the arts was carefully cultivated—in calligraphy and painting, in costume, in music and the dance, even in competitions for the invention of new perfumes. Yet the final chapters of the long and complex *Tale of Genji* are tinged with melancholy, with a Buddhist sense of the dreamlike unreality of this world. The mood of that Japanese phrase *mono no aware* (pronounced mono no ah-wahr-ay) has been said to correspond to the Latin poet's *lacrimae rerum,* the tears of things, or the pathos of things. *Mono no aware* involved a sensitivity to the beauties of nature (cherry blossoms and autumn leaves, for instance) together with sorrow at their evanescence, at the inevitability of their passing away. For paintings that evoke the mood of *The Tale of Genji,* we turn in the next chapter to the art of the narrative scroll.

Early Heian period (Japan) Nikko, the Sun Bodhisattva

Suiko period (Japan) Miroku Bosatsu
(see also page 165)

Artist Unknown *Gohimitsu Bosatsu* ("The Secret Five")

13
THE NARRATIVE SKILLS

There are many references in poetry, and in the tales and diaries, to screens and hand scrolls in the households of the nobility in the Fujiwara times. The colorful and decorative paintings that depicted the gentle landscape of Japan and seasonal activities of the people were even then called *Yamato-e* ("Japanese picture"). By extension the term came to include the most characteristic of Japanese inventions, the narrative scroll, or *e-maki*.

Although in China, illustrations of stories and poems, and descriptions of seasonal festivities, occur in the hand scroll format, it is the long, horizontal landscape scrolls that are among the supreme achievements of

Chinese art. As the scroll unrolls from right to left, one may imagine oneself traveling along mountain paths, or by river boat, or climbing the height to a remote temple. In the paintings it is not a human situation that is being explored—it is the nature of Nature itself.

In Japan, although the landscape setting may enrich the narrative scroll, the emphasis is on the activities of men and women, nobles and peasants, warriors and priests, a vision of the Western Paradise, or the fear of ghosts and of hell—in short, the varieties of human experience, the movement of life itself. In the unfolding drama of the narrative scroll, the artists of medieval Japan devised a form that is unique in the art of the world. It is a fortunate accident that fragments from one of the earliest examples of the narrative tradition, *The Genji Monogatari*, present passages of text and illustrations from the world's first novel. Made about a century after Murasaki Shikibu was writing, this scroll originally may have been composed of a hundred individual scenes. Each was preceded by a section of text written in an elegant running hand on beautifully decorated paper sprinkled with gold and silver in endless variation. Of the paintings, only nineteen have survived. They are kept in the Tokugawa Museum in Nagoya and in the Goto Museum in Tokyo.

In the scene reproduced on page 197, two beautiful daughters of Lady Tamakatsura are playing *go*. They have decided that the winner in two out of three games will claim the cherry tree in the garden for her own. We see Himegami, in a white costume, but only from the back. The head of her sister opposite is obscured by the rolled-up curtains, so that we see only a suggestion of her long black hair, her voluminous costume, and her right hand moving a piece on the gameboard. Two young girls in attendance "very beautiful in the evening light"[1] are seated on the verandah beyond the cherry tree. At the lower right, Genji's supposed grandson, Kaoru, hopelessly in love with Himegami, looks on unobserved. Rich color harmonies set the key for the painting. The flowing curves of costume, the verticals and diagonals of architectural detail, and the sparkle of cherry blossoms are also elements in an enchanting composition. But it is an enchantment vaguely tinged with melancholy in this painting in yellows, greens, reds, and brown. In an earlier picture, the sorrow of Prince Genji, as he sits watching the dying Lady Murasaki, is translated into muted red-violet, faded browns, and silvery gray. Autumn grasses beyond the verandah are bending toward this somber scene, the evocation of an altogether different mood.

Two characteristic artistic conventions are evident in the *Genji* scroll: the roofless house (or "blown-away roof") that enables us to observe what is going on inside, and the masklike faces ("straight-line eyes and hooked-line noses"). Sei Shonagon observed in her *Pillow Book* that "among things that lose by being painted" are "men or women who are praised in romances as being beautiful." Perhaps aristocratic readers preferred such abstract masks to more individualized and less satisfactory representations of their favorite heroes and heroines. In any case, the masklike faces correspond to the courtly decorum that was supposed to conceal too obvious emotional involvement.

As to the technique of painting, composition and drawing were indicated in ink on paper, then covered with opaque color. Finally the original drawing as remembered, or sometimes revised, was sketched in again, in ink. In the head of the young man at the lower right some of the opaque color has disappeared. We can see the first drawing and a slightly different placing of the line that represents the final drawing after the application of color. The whole project, estimated by a Japanese scholar[2] to have once been about 450 feet long and probably in twenty rolls, was supervised by a professional court artist, with talented amateurs as assistants, presumably ladies of the court, for the application of color and for the superb passages of calligraphy.

It has been observed that if the paintings in the *Genji* resemble stills from some gorgeous motion picture, *The Heiji Monogatari,* painted a century or so later, is more like an actual film itself. One of the treasures of the Museum of Fine Arts in Boston and the most famous of the narrative scrolls outside of Japan, *The Heiji Monogatari* vividly describes a dramatic event in the struggle of clans for power during thirty years of bloody civil war preceding the Kamakura shogunate.

In the color detail reproduced on pages 198 and 199, we see the drive and panic of rebellion. Hundreds of soldiers on foot or on horseback are projected across the scroll as they storm the palace. They seize the ex-emperor and bundle him into a heavy state carriage. They set the palace on fire. The troops regroup and continue moving forward. The

Conclusion of
The Heiji Monogatari
Emaki scroll (detail)

scroll ends with the single figure of a commander on horseback preceded by a foot soldier with his great bow ready to shoot. No text interrupts the action; there is drama enough in the visual experience. Text precedes and follows the broad sweep of the painting. Colors are rich and deep—greens, orange, and blacks predominate with black used in a variety of ways. This tumult of soldiers and their victims is set against empty space except where the solid walls of the palace slow the action. Although it is the movement of the whole group that compels our attention, there is much extraordinary detail in the expression of faces, the depiction of armor, the staccato of weapons, while the flames and smoke of the burning palace are probably unsurpassed in all of art.

By the end of this civil war, a new age of feudalism had begun. But much of Kyoto was destroyed, the great temple of Todai-ji at Nara was burned down, and the countryside was devastated. Reformers appeared in the Buddhist establishment, teachers and preachers concerned for the people in their poverty and despair. Legends and stories of these influential priests and their temples, of salvation and rebirth in the Western Paradise—the Pure Land—along with cautionary tales about the horrors of hell, all provided subjects for the narrative painters.

Artist Unknown *The Frolicking Animals and People* (detail)

A third famous scroll of the twelfth century, *The Frolicking Animals and People,* is still kept at the temple where it was made, Kōzan-ji in Kyoto. Not painted in opaque watercolor like the *Genji* or *The Heiji Monogatari,* the four rolls of the scroll are set down with brush and ink on paper, a witty comment on human folly. Because monk-artists who made paintings for the Tendai and Shingon sects were familiar with ink-line copybooks as models, they became experienced in a technique easily adapted to these humorous and slightly irreverent ink paintings.

In the section reproduced on the preceeding page, one must admire the skillful brush that indicates the backbone curves of the two rabbits, the rhythmic flow of water, the harsher angles of rocks, and the very Japanese flowers and grasses in the foreground. Another part shows monkeys worshiping a frog, seated in the position of meditation, against a banana-leaf halo. There is lively observation of both animal and human behavior, and no text at all.

Artist Unknown
Yuzu Nembutsu Engi: Ryonin, Fox, and Falcon (detail)

A long *engi* (history or legends of a temple, as in *Shigi-san-engi*), comprised of two scrolls is called the *Yuzu-nembutsu Engi (The Efficacy of Repeated Invocations to the Amida Buddha)*. Scroll one is in the collection of the Art Institute of Chicago; scroll two at the Cleveland Museum of Art. Other scrolls exist in Japan with stories about the priest, Ryonin, and the powerful Nembutsu sect of Pure Land Buddhism that he founded. But the *Yuzu-nembutsu Engi* are the earliest of the pictorial versions of this subject.

The second roll opens with an engaging painting of birds and animals inquiring if they may join in devotion to Amida Buddha. The priest, Ryonin, with the fox and the falcon suggests an Eastern version of Saint Francis of Assisi. In another episode, a nun worships before a household altar. We see the arrangement of hanging scrolls on the wall. The central scroll represents a *Raigo*—the Buddha and two Bodhisattvas descending from the Western Paradise. Above the heads of the nun's two

Artist Unknown
Yuzu Nembutsu Engi: Raigo, Nun, and Attendants (detail)

Artist Unknown
Yuzu Nembutsu Engi:
Demons (detail)

Artist Unknown
Guardian Figure

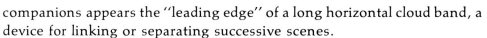

companions appears the "leading edge" of a long horizontal cloud band, a device for linking or separating successive scenes.

A third episode illustrates the story of a village chief in a time of pestilence. He made a list of members of his family, old and young, who would keep up a perpetual recitation of the *yuzu nembutsu* in hopes of avoiding the plague. One night he dreamed that demons and intruders came to his door. He told them they should not come in, that his list was on the altar. They stayed at the door but asked to see the list, whereupon the spirits with a delighted appearance put their seals under the names. The village chief told them he had a daughter living in a different place and wished to add her name which they did not allow. His dream ended there. The following morning he looked into the list and found a seal mark under each name. The dream proved truly prophetic, for all members of the family remained in good health while the daughter who was away died of the pestilence.[3] Notice with what ingenuity the artist has varied the feet or claws of the ghostly intruders, and the way in which the unswept hair suggests the supernatural. You can see one source of inspiration for the Halloween-like ghosts in the splendid warrior Guardian, an example of temple sculpture now in the Art Institute of Chicago.

Anyone who is familiar with the classics of modern Japanese film making, *Rashomon, Ugetsu,* or the *Gate of Hell,* for instance, will realize

Still photograph from *Ugetsu*

Still photograph from *Rashomon*

that the spoken words, like the text in most narrative scrolls, are infinitely less important than the visual images. "If I could have said it in words," Kurasawa, who directed *Rashomon*, is quoted as saying, "I wouldn't have gone to the trouble and expense of making a film."[4] Kurasawa's film of 1975, *Dersu Uzala—the Hunter*, movingly presents traditional Japanese themes, the changing seasons, and man's relation to Nature. This twentieth century story of a Siberian nomad and a Russian surveyor in the wilderness areas of northeast Asia, is told in color on a wide screen with powerful and sometimes poignant images that recall to those who know them the narrative scrolls of medieval Japan.

14

ZEN, SESSHU, AND THE WAY OF TEA

Most of the Japanese paintings we have encountered so far—Buddhist paintings or narrative scrolls—have been in color. In this monochrome ink painting we see a Zen priest mending his robe in the morning sunlight. The "rapturous torrential sweeps of dark ink"[1] in the robe are contrasted with the delicacy of the thread, and of the hand that holds the needle. Painted by Kao in the first half of the fourteenth century, "water and ink" was a new way of working for Japanese artists.

A photograph made in 1972 points out that in spite of modern industrialization, the Zen way of life survives in the monasteries of Japan today, sometimes preserving the medieval ways almost intact, sometimes

Kao Choyo: *Priest Sewing*
under the Morning Sun

Zen Monk Sewing Photograph

with adjustments to the modern world. (It might, however, surprise the reader to learn that there are more young people in training in Zen monasteries in the United States today than there are in Japan.[2])

A second visual comparison contrasts a famous painting about a legendary figure of Chinese Buddhism asleep with his tiger and a brush drawing by Rembrandt. The Chinese painting is set down in a very free brush manner developed by certain artists of Southern Sung times, a style that was adopted by Zen painters in Japan. In a strange way this engaging Chinese painting seems closer in feeling to the Rembrandt brush drawing than to a formal symmetrically arranged Buddhist icon like the *Secret Five* on page 179. And if there is a smile on the face of the tiger, the lady in Rembrandt's drawing sleeps peacefully on the page beside him.

About this particular drawing, the Rembrandt scholar, Otto Benesch, observes:

> The drawing was done very quickly, and the brush-strokes are like sword-cuts, yet with infinite firmness form is seized and fixed, without any need of pentimenti.[3]

Attributed to Shih K'o
The Second Zen Patriarch

Rembrandt *A Girl Sleeping
(study after Hendrickje)* Dutch

And in an interpretation of atmosphere and space one finds parallels to Zen:

> The intention of thick lines in Rembrandt's late drawings is not to make a heavily-marked separation from the mysterious medium of space. On the contrary, it means all the more intensive union with the atmosphere. The atmosphere is, so to speak, banked up on the figures' outlines and becomes visible in dark borders. The figures on the other hand change their substance and become embodiments of atmospheric space, now more a metaphysical medium than a physical one.[4]

Sometimes a detail of brushwork, lifted out of the context of subject matter may force us to see the character of the brushstrokes in a new way as shown below. The possibility has even been suggested that Rembrandt may have seen Oriental ink paintings in Holland, a country that had an active trade with the Far East.[5]

Details from Shih K'o and from Rembrandt

In a third comparison, the painting in oils is by the Spanish artist, Francisco de Zurbarán (1598–1664). The clear yellows and orange of the fruit stand out against a dark table and background. Although the setting appears to be a domestic interior, some sense of spiritual or religious meaning seems to pervade the nearly symmetrical composition, arranged almost as if it were an offering on an altar. The oranges are enclosed, held within their basket; the lemons on their plate; the water within the cup. The atmosphere is one of quiet intensity.

Mu Ch'i, painter and Ch'an priest, lived at a temple near Hangchou in the thirteenth century. He painted the *Six Persimmons* in ink and water on paper fourteen and a half inches wide. Perhaps, in contrast to the Zurbarán, we notice first the undefined space, the sense of movement in

Francisco de Zurbarán
Still Life: Lemons, Oranges and a Rose Spanish

Mu Ch'i *Six Persimmons*

the surrounding atmosphere. This is no still life, no "dead nature" as in that French phrase, *nature morte.* The persimmons seem to have a life of their own and to share in our breathing space. We notice the weight of the darkest and largest fruit, and how the tones grow lighter as they are placed farther from the center. The stems, so black, so crisply written, have the look of Chinese characters. In its silence, understatement, and directness, the painting is very Zen. The persimmons are just *there,* in all their persimmon-ness. And it is, in its own way, as much a religious painting as a representation in color and gold of Buddha descending from heaven with Bodhisattvas and angels.

How was it that the ink-painting styles of Ch'an in China—styles we have glimpsed in the *Second Zen Patriarch* and the *Six Persimmons*—came to be adopted by so many painters in Japan in the fifteenth and sixteenth centuries? What was "Ch'an," a name derived from the Sanskrit *dhyana* meaning meditation, and more familiar to us in its Japanese form as Zen?

Ch'an was the one sect of Buddhism in China that retained its influence after the fall of the T'ang dynasty. While its teachings reflect the traditional Buddhist search for enlightenment, it is also tinged with the commonsense of Confucianism: no work, no food. The monks mended their own robes, grew their own vegetables, cared for their own temples. But Ch'an is also deeply infused with the insights of Taoism. Art and poetry and philosophy came under the influence of Ch'an temples in the Sung dynasty. In foreign trade, the Ch'an monks were influential. They went to teach in Japan; they entertained Japanese priests in their own temples; and they advised government officials about commercial enterprises, including the export of paintings and ceramics. Some of these Chinese paintings found their way into the distinguished collections of the Ashikaga shoguns who not only were adepts of Zen discipline and the tea ceremony but also were powerful patrons and builders of Zen temples in Japan. Thus Chinese art traveled to Japan with the second great wave of Buddhist influence that came in the fifteenth and sixteenth centuries.

The close tie between art and Zen rises from the very heart of the discipline itself. Among its distinguishing features are the belief that the Buddha nature is within oneself, and the conviction that there is no special merit in knowledge of the scriptures, in images, or ceremony, no Western Paradise for easy salvation. According to the Zen teachings, it is not through logical thought but in a moment of sudden illumination that one experiences ultimate truth, a realization that there is no separation of man and nature, that subject and object are one, that the Buddha nature is both within and without. After this experience one returns to the world as it is, seeing the world with new vision but finding that "the mountains are still mountains, the waters still waters."

For the traveler in Japan, one of the most moving, most surprising and sobering of visual experiences may be the "dry rock" garden of a Zen temple. At Ryoan-ji in Kyoto one views in astonished silence a garden of

Ryoan-ji Garden Kyoto, Photograph

raked white gravel, of five groups of rocks, and of open space. Without trees or plants, it is a garden within limits yet apparently limitless. Some see the rocks as islands in a sea of raked gravel. Some imagine a mother tiger bringing her cubs across a stream. But somehow, in a mysterious way, the garden induces silence and contemplation. The familiar is made extraordinary in this "ideal landscape, this garden for the mind," although the gravel is still gravel and the rocks are still rocks.

SESSHU TOYO *(1420–1506)*

The most influential painter to develop within the Zen tradition during the Ashikaga shogunate had lived since the age of twelve in a Zen temple far from Kyoto. By 1440, Sesshu Toyo was a novice at Shokoku-ji, the great Zen monastery built by the Ashikaga shoguns at Kyoto. He was to remain there for the next twenty years as priest and administrator, learning Chinese and studying ink monochrome painting under Shubun, the most influential teacher in the capital. While at Shokoku-ji, Sesshu would have had access to the Chinese paintings of the Sung and Yuan periods in the celebrated collection of the Ashikaga shogun, Yoshimasa (1449–1490), a remarkable learning opportunity for any artist.

In 1467, Sesshu was privileged to see China at first hand, as part of the trade mission sent by the Lords of Ouchi, in whose family temple he had served since he left Kyoto and Shokoku-ji. Treated with distinction in Zen monasteries in China, he even seems to have been well received in the capital, where he came in contact with some of the Ming court painters. But it was not from the artists of China that he learned most. It was, he said, from the mountains and rivers, the strange plants, trees, birds, beasts, and men with their different customs. For him these were the real paintings of China. By 1468, perhaps earlier, Sesshu was back again in Japan. But civil war had destroyed the buildings of Shokoku-ji, along with much of Kyoto. Held in great esteem, especially after his travels in China, Sesshu lived the rest of his life in Western Honshu, or on Kyushu.

> Sesshu's brush is natural and spontaneous
> It seems as though his very blood were ink
> And everything he touches turns to painting.[6]

Eighteen years after his return from China, Sesshu painted the Mori scroll, extending more than fifty feet in length, in ink and faint color. It was a remembrance of China, a continuously evolving sequence of landscape motifs and of the changing seasons. It was a brilliant tour de force and generally considered to be Sesshu's masterpiece, executed when he was sixty-six years old. The scroll opens with sharp, rocky forms set down in the decisive "ax-cut" strokes that recall Ma Yuan. As the scroll is unrolled, we see from time to time a Zen priest and his attendant moving along pathways that help to guide us through the landscape. At one point we seem to cross open water where fishing boats are anchored close to a village overhung with willows. The time is now summer. Later

Sesshu Toyo
Long Landscape Scroll (detail)

we come to a wine shop and a gathering of people beneath a tangle of rock forms and tree patterns. The journey comes to a close in an austere and snowy landscape. Variety and continuity are the miracle of this scroll, along with the contrast of sharply accented masses against dissolving mist and water.

In contrast to the sustained power of the Mori scroll (difficult to present in reproduction), *Winter Landscape* is a small painting only 18¼ × 11½ inches in size. If ever a brushmark could be described as a sword stroke, it would certainly be the intense vertical line descending from the mountain height into the wintry landscape. Below that sharp dividing line, a single traveler climbs the steep road to a temple half lost in the cold deep snow.

Sesshu Toyo *Winter Landscape*

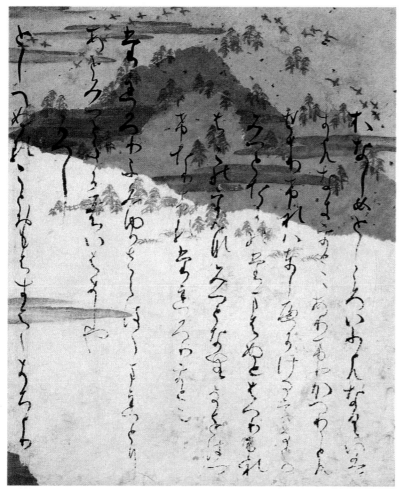

Section from the *Ise-shu*

Artist Unknown *The Daughters of Lady
Tamakatsura Playing Go,* (detail from *The
Tale of Genji* scroll)

Artist Unknown
The Burning of Sanjo Palace
(detail from *The Heiji Monogatari Emaki* scroll)

Water Pot: Shino Ware

Ninsei *Tea Bowls*

There were many important artists painting in ink in the fifteenth and sixteenth centuries, but Sesshu was an artist of extraordinary versatility. He painted screens in ink and watercolor that are his own adaption of Chinese Ming dynasty "bird and flower" paintings, enlarging details of flowering plants with enormous decorative effect. He painted one of the most celebrated scenic areas of Japan, Ama-no-hashidate, proving that Japanese artists could find subjects in their own land without constantly copying the landscapes of a China they had never seen.

But the most mysterious, the most Zen of all Sesshu's paintings is surely the *haboku* (splashed ink) landscape acquired from Shokoku-ji early in this century by the Tokyo National Museum. Sesshu made the small painting, mounted as a hanging scroll, for his devoted student,

Sesshu Toyo
"Haboku" Landscape

Soen, and wrote the inscription for him directly above the painting. A rocky promontory, a distant vertical cliff or mountain, a wine shop with its flag, and at the lower right, a slender boat, all enveloped in mist—in space that is formless and yet "is the source of all form." The contrast of crisp black brushmarks against an enveloping atmosphere combines the painting skills of a master with the special insights of Zen Buddhism.

THE WAY OF TEA

Tea did not become commonplace in the West until the eighteenth century. Nowadays when we think of a tea party, we are liable to think of pretty cups and saucers, little sandwiches and cakes, a hum of conversation, perhaps candlelight reflected from polished silver. Teaspoons are usually identical in pattern. Guests enter the room without bowing their heads.

But tea had been commonly used in China since the T'ang dynasty. "Brick tea" was known in Heian Japan. Powdered tea, introduced to

*Garden Approach
to a Tea Hut* Kyoto, Photograph

Japan by Zen monks returning from China, was used to keep drowsy monks awake during the long hours of sitting in meditation. And the tea ceremony of Japan is steeped in the spirit of Zen. First developed by tea masters for their patrons, it was Sen-no-Rikyu (1521–91) who developed the classic tea ceremony, its form, and appropriate setting.

A simple garden path led to a small teahouse, not more than ten feet square, probably with a thatched roof, a doorway so low one had to bow one's head to enter it (a sign of humility), tatami matting on the floor, and paper windows allowing a subdued light. In the alcove, or *tokonoma*, was hung a single vertical scroll. The "splashed ink" landscape by Sesshu in the Tokyo National Museum, or a calligraphy scroll, would have been appropriate for thoughtful contemplation, set off by a modest spray or a single flower in a pottery or bamboo container. Here the host received a little group of friends—no more than four or five guests—serving them some delicately prepared food and frothy green tea whipped up with a

Tokonoma:
"Tai-An" at Myoki-An, Photograph

bamboo whisk in water that had been boiled in an iron kettle over a charcoal fire. Reverence, harmony, purity, and tranquility, these were the words used to describe the atmosphere of quiet formality, and sensitive appreciation of the utensils (no matching patterns!) and the carefully composed surroundings.

Garden design, architecture, painting, flower arranging, ceramics, and various crafts—metalwork, lacquer baskets, bamboo, paper, and textiles—entered into this harmonious whole. So the tea masters whose tastes were formed by Zen came to have a very real influence on the craftsmen whose work they discovered and developed and, eventually, through their discriminating choices on the taste of the Japanese people.

The discerning eye of a tea master might find a peasant bowl from Korea as appropriate for the use of an honored guest as a precious porcelain teabowl from China. It has been pointed out that many a *daimyo* accepted a simple tea utensil from his lord in preference to a landed estate.[7] And even today, a simple object that was once in the possession of a famous tea master commands a fabulous price in Japan.

What follows is a small selection of ceramics in the "tea taste." Among them are storage jars made of pottery with natural glazes from the "Six Old Kilns," jars made originally for farmers to store seeds or water, and admired by the tea masters for their earthy coloring and strong, spontaneous shapes. The Shigaraki jar from the late fourteenth or fifteenth century is crisply inscribed with a lattice-fence pattern on the shoulder. In a sixteenth-century water jar of Shino ware made for the tea

Water Jar: Tamba Ware   *Storage Jar: Shigaraki Ware*

*Dish with Design of
Three Wild Geese in Flight:
Gray Shino Ware*

Donyu "Tamamushi"

ceremony, reproduced on page 200, the thick glaze is painted in iron-oxide slip, with a free version of that same lattice pattern. To the eye trained in the tea taste, this piece is altogether extraordinary in its controlled freedom.

The shallow bowl above, another type of Shino ware, is decorated with three cranes in white slip on a "mouse-gray" ground.

With the black *raku* teabowl we come to an artist-potter who can be identified. Made at Kyoto by Donyu (1599–1656), the bowl is named *Tamamushi* ("Golden Beetle"). Donyu's father was patronized by the tea master Sen-no-Rikyu, and was the founder of a family tradition that has lasted to the present day. *Raku* bowls are not coil-built, not thrown on the wheel, but shaped by hand, thus preserving the individuality of the

Dish: Mino Ware, Oribe type

potter, and they were fired at low temperatures in a simple kiln that could be set up in any garden. (Such a *raku* kiln is set up from time to time in a garden next door to this writer, right in the midst of the city of Cleveland.) *Raku* bowls, indeed all of the tea-ceremony wares, have had an enormous influence on contemporary potters in the United States and in England.

The Oribe-ware plate in the Freer Gallery was designed in the taste of Sen-no-Rikyu's student, Furuta Oribe. It is clearly a departure from earlier wares in its bold asymmetry and lively design. And the handsome seventeenth-century tea bowls by Nonomura Ninsei (1596–1660) reproduced on page 200 with their elegant use of color on a white ground make a bridge from the earlier and more austere tea wares in the Zen taste to the emerging Decorative Style.

15
THE DECORATIVE STYLE
Two Pairs of Artists

Japanese art seems always to be presenting us with contrasts: melancholy or humorous, understated or flamboyant, influenced by China or unmistakably Japanese. In the time of the Ashikaga shoguns, as we have seen, the Zen taste was dominant. But the essentially Japanese love of color, of exquisite detail in the old *Yamato-e* way of painting, continued to flourish, especially among artists close to the court. It was a taste that was fully consonant with the Chinese tradition of decorative painting, especially of birds and flowers. This colorful, decorative quality so often used in Japan on a small scale was suddenly, at the beginning of a new age, enlarged and revitalized on the walls and folding screens of the fortresses and pleasure palaces built by three extraordinary military leaders. These generals, these dictators, who succeeded in pacifying and unifying Japan after years of civil war, were Nobunaga (1534–1582), Hideyoshi (1537–1598), sometimes called the Napoleon of Japan, and Tokugawa Ieyasu (1542–1616), who established, under a feudal government, a peace that was to last for the next two hundred and fifty years.

Nobunaga, determined to subdue the warring clans, built a castle at Azuchi in 1576 (later destroyed) in a style of architecture that was new to Japan. He was the first military leader to make use of the firearms introduced to Japan by the Portuguese—actually by shipwrecked Portuguese sailors in 1543. New weapons also called for new ways of defensive fortification, with massive stone construction for walls and dungeon, and with multiple-roofed living quarters on the upper floors.

Members of the Kano family of painters were commissioned to provide wall panels and screens for many of the new fortresses and palaces. Although admired for their disciplined Chinese brushwork (as in the illustration on the next page), they often combined their Chinese ink style with gold grounds and color. The subject matter of the Kano painters in the sixteenth and seventeenth centuries has been well described by Sir George Sansom:

Himeji (White Heron Castle), Photograph

Attributed to
Kano Motonobu
Mandarin Ducks (detail)

On the walls, mostly of bright gold, there are blue-eyed tigers prowling through groves of bamboo, or multi-coloured *shishi*—mythical beasts like lions, but amiable and curly-haired—that gambol among peonies against a golden background. There are gorgeous landscapes, thick with old pines and blossoming plum-trees, where bright birds perch on fantastic rocks or float amid ripples of deep blue.[1]

In this chapter, however, we turn to two pairs of artists born about a hundred years apart—artists who concerned themselves with Japanese subject matter treated in a more distinctively Japanese style. Of these the best-known are Tawaraya Sotatsu and Ogata Korin. We will also consider briefly Sotatsu's friend—in some ways his guide and patron—Hon-ami Koetsu, and along with Korin, his brother Ogata Kenzan.

HON-AMI KOETSU *(1558–1637* and
TAWARAYA SOTATSU *(c. 1570–after 1640)*

It is with unfailing delight that this writer recalls an afternoon spent in a quiet room of the Berlin Museum, in the *Museum für Ostasiatische Kunst,* looking at, or perhaps one should say, absorbing a choice album of thirty-six small paintings. About six by seven inches in size, these album leaves, called *shikishi,* were decorated with paintings in gold and silver attributed to Sotatsu, and written over, in his graceful cursive hand, by

Calligraphy by Koetsu
Decoration attributed to
Sotatsu *Shikishi*

Koetsu. In a number of collaborative works by this pair of artists, no one is quite sure who did what. Koetsu may sometimes have had a hand in the paintings. More likely, he knew how to call upon the creative gifts of Sotatsu for the preparation of those enchanting backgrounds. The famous *Deer Scroll* is painted in thin washes of gold and silver. Over groupings of deer, moving or at rest, Koetsu wrote out poems from the *Shinkokinshu.* The deer illustrate no specific poems; they provide a mood or musical background, as it were, for the placing of the short lyrics or *waka.* These two examples—the *Album* in Berlin and the *Deer Scroll* (half of it in the United States, the other half in Japan)—can only begin to suggest the variety and fascination of the many collaborative works by Sotatsu and Koetsu, or their circle, in which painting and poetry are perfectly harmonized.

Born into a family with a long tradition as connoisseurs of swords at the court, Koetsu was devoted to the No theatre, trained in the tea ceremony, a poet, and especially well known as a calligrapher, "one of the three best brush artists of his time." He was a cultivated amateur,

rather than a professional artist. Koetsu designed lacquer. He interested himself in ceramics, learning how to make *raku* tea bowls. The dozen or so teabowls that can be ascribed to Koetsu are among the most famous in all Japan. Such choice teabowls were given their own names, *White Rain, Autumn Showers,* and *Fuji San* (Mount Fuji):

Hon-ami Koetsu
Tea Bowl: Kyoto Raku Ware

In 1615, Koetsu founded an artists' colony northwest of Kyoto—*Takagamine* by name. It became a community of artists and craftsmen, among whom were papermakers and potters, woodworkers, lacquer makers, textile workers, brush makers, and painters, with houses for their families, workshops, studios, and temples. Here Koetsu advised and encouraged some of the ablest craftsmen of his time in their individual and cooperative enterprises.

Finally, Koetsu had a large share in a revival of the arts of Heian Japan, especially painting, calligraphy, and poetry. The poems that he inscribed in his graceful hand were usually chosen from the old anthologies and from such tales as *The Ise Monogatari* and *The Genji Monogatari.* Koetsu was honoring in this way the traditional aristocratic tastes of Kyoto at a time when a more bustling, commercial society was establishing itself in the new town of Edo, which we know as Tokyo.

Much is uncertain about the life of Sotatsu. He apparently came from a prosperous family of merchants, and became head of a fan-making establishment, known as the *Tawaraya,* in Kyoto. He began his professional life as a skilled craftsman and not as a member of an official school or family of painters. But the *Tawaraya* became more than a fan shop. It was a busy studio workshop, filling commissions for fans, for the underpainting of scrolls and *shikishi,* and for the large screen paintings, which might be compared to commissions for mural paintings in Italy.

Attributed to Tawaraya Sotatsu *Decorated Fans*

Some of the fan paintings have been preserved because they were mounted on screens. We can see at once with what skill Sotatsu composed his forms within the special shape of the folding fan. Sometimes the directions of the composition seem related to the sticks of the

Attributed to Tawaraya Sotatsu
Decorated Fans (detail)

fan; sometimes the composition moves horizontally in flowing curves from right to left as it might on a hand scroll.

> In autumn the wild geese cry
> And chrysanthemums are in flower,
> Yet how pleasant to dwell
> By the sea in spring
> On the Beach of Sumiyoshi.[2]

This poem is inscribed on a small album leaf attributed to Sotatsu. We can see in the illustration on page 217 that the colors are rich against the gold ground, with flat tones and patterns and a delicate adjustment of the rhythmic calligraphy to the pictorial composition. We may notice also the soft watercolor quality in the trees and a foreground rock where colors have been allowed to run together with a casual effect.

The wet-in-wet watercolor technique seems to derive from Sotatsu's skill in painting with Chinese ink and water with a wonderful freedom of handling. Ink dropped into a puddle of paler ink will produce chance effects, happy accidents, that the artist can use to his own advantage. This technique, translated into color, is considered one of the innovations of Sotatsu. Color is dripped into underpainted areas that are still wet, a technique that is given the special name *tarashikomi.* In the *Poppies,* a

fresh and appealing composition on a pair of screens in the Museum of Fine Arts in Boston, this technique, in certain places, allows the gold ground to glimmer through a transparent watercolor wash into which a second color has been diffused. The golden screens of Momoyama and Edo times, incidentally, were made of small squares of very thin gold leaf mounted on heavy paper. Sotatsu was indeed a master who understood his materials—ink, paper, gold leaf, and color, whether transparent or opaque. He lets the materials themselves enchant us, lets us see their expressive qualities, their infinite variety.

That Sotatsu was also a master of rhythmic movement you can see in a splendid pair of screens brought to the United States from Japan in 1906 by Charles Freer. The *Waves at Matsushima* are now in the collection of the Freer Gallery of Art, a part of the Smithsonian Institution in Washington, so we may say that in a sense these screens belong to all Americans. The Japanese consider them among the greatest of their masterpieces now in collections outside Japan. In the detail on page 218, you can see the way the waves surge and eddy, drive forward, crest, and break against the rocky islets. The curious form in the left screen is a sandbar just barely awash. Above, a long, golden sand spit supports a pair of windblown pines. We notice also the free and expressive way in which tones of blue and green and warm brown indicate the forms of the small islands.

OGATA KORIN *(1658–1716)* and OGATA KENZAN *(1663–1743)*

Screens like the one reproduced here, by an unknown artist, suggest the richness and variety of textile patterns and costume in the Momoyama

Tawaraya Sotatsu
The Waves at Matsushima
(see also page 218)

and Edo periods. This representation of garments on a clothes rack, belongs in a group with the delightful title "Whose Sleeves?" The screen is one of a pair appropriately kept in the Musée Guimet in Paris, which like Kyoto, has been for centuries a center of the arts, including the art of fashion.

Korin and his brother Kenzan were sons of a wealthy textile merchant in Kyoto, Ogata being the family name. Their father was also a

Artist Unknown
Tagasode ("Whose Sleeves?")

painter, calligrapher, and expert in the tea ceremony; his establishment, the *Kariganeya,* had been founded by a grandfather whose sister had married Koetsu. Concerned with the design, weaving, and dyeing of superb silks and brocades, the *Kariganeya* flourished, patronized by the great ladies of their time.

Born just a hundred years after Koetsu, Korin looked back with admiration and respect to the two distinguished artists, Koetsu and Sotatsu, who were connected with his family by marriage and by aesthetic tastes. Japan was now at peace. Merchants and townspeople were prospering. The brothers lived a privileged life in a household devoted to poetry and painting, to the No theatre, the tea ceremony, and music. Korin was regarded as a playboy and a spendthrift, enjoying life to the full. Kenzan, four years younger, was of a quieter nature, devoted to Zen Buddhism and to books.

When their father died, an elder brother inherited the business, but Korin and Kenzan were each provided with considerable wealth. Korin soon spent his share and turned to painting as a source of support. The years in which he made his name as an artist, the Genroku era (1688–1704), were among the most dazzling in Japanese history, a time of elegance and of creativity in Kyoto, and in the new and competitive city of Edo.

Korin recorded his admiration for Sotatsu in his own variation on Sotatsu's *Waves at Matsushima,* kept now in the Museum of Fine Arts in Boston. If Sotatsu's method of pictorial organization was based on the shape of the folding fan, Korin's composition seems determined by his experience with round fans—he tends to dispose forms within circular schemes.[3] His sure sense of placement and of intervals probably derives in part from an experience of fitting designs into the round shape of a fan, or into the curves and circles of textile patterns.

The fan with chrysanthemums against a stream on page 221 seems like a motif in the opening measures of a symphony, a motif that appears on a grander scale, more developed on a pair of golden screens in Cleveland.

In *Chrysanthemums by a Stream,* one of a pair of screens reproduced on page 221, the motif of a single branching stalk has been repeated with variations, growing now from the near bank of the stream, now from the further bank. The crisp white flowers are in slight relief, molded in powdered clamshell. The blossoms are shown only full face, in profile, or from directly behind. The painter never loses control of the effect he is aiming at through involvement in the many possible variations of form and position of the flowers. For the same reason, colors are limited to the gold ground, a lighter yellow-green, a deeper blue-green, and the blue-black stream. Sherman Lee has pointed out how clearly the waves are like a textile pattern, that it is almost as if the screens were a collage made of real plants against a wave-patterned textile that has been applied flat to the gold ground.[4]

Attributed to Tawaraya Sotatsu *On the Beach at Sumiyoshi*

Tawaraya Sotatsu *The Waves at Matsushima* (detail)

Ogata Korin *Irises and Bridge*

Ogata Kenzan *Set of Five Plates*

Ogata Korin *Chrysanthemums by a Stream*

Ikeno Taiga *Lan-t'ing* (detail)

Ogata Korin *Waves*

But the favorite motifs of Korin never became fixed in a consistent pattern. Compare the quiet elegance of waves, held within an ornamental shoreline of the chrysanthemum screen with the dramatic surging water painted in Chinese ink on a gold ground reproduced here.

A passage in the *Ise Monogatari* provided the motif for a number of important works by Korin.

Once a certain man decided that it was useless for him to remain in the capital. With one or two old friends, he set out toward the east in search of a province in which to settle. Since none of the party knew the way, they blundered ahead as best they could, until in time they arrived at a place called Yatsuhashi in Mikawa Province. (It was a spot where the waters of a river branched into eight channels, each with a bridge, and thus it had come to be called Yatsuhashi—"Eight Bridges.") Dismounting to sit under a tree near this marshy area, they ate a meal of parched rice. Someone glanced at the clumps of irises that were blooming luxuriantly in the swamp. "Compose a poem on the subject, 'A Traveler's Sentiments,' beginning each line with a syllable from the word 'iris' [*kakitsubata*]," he said. The man recited,

Karagoromo	I have a beloved wife,
Kitsutsu narenishi	Familiar as the skirt
Tsuma shi areba	Of a well-worn robe,
Harubaru kinuru	And so this distant journeying
Tabi o shi zo omou.	Fills my heart with grief.

They all wept onto their dried rice until it swelled with the moisture.[5]

One illustration of the scene is this hanging scroll complete with the traveler, his two companions, the rice bowl, a bridge, and clumps of iris. On page 218, in one of a pair of splendid screens on a gold ground in the Metropolitan Museum in New York, we see only the iris along with sections of the bridge. Finally, in a pair of famous screens in Tokyo, the

Ogata Korin *Yatsuhashi*

Ogata Korin *Irises*

bridges disappear—only the iris remain. But for a Japanese viewer, the poem is still implied. For us there is poetry in the iris themselves, their rhythmic repetitions and fresh, spontaneous quality.

This motif of the iris was often used by Korin and his followers, but nowhere more effectively on a small scale than in his design for a lacquer writing box now in the Tokyo National Museum. Black lacquer and gold lacquer, mother-of-pearl and pewter, were played against each other. Here Korin brings together the skills of designer, craftsman, and painter in a masterpiece of the decorative arts.

Although less extravagant by nature than his older brother, there came a time when Kenzan, too, could no longer live on his inheritance, and was forced to look for a source of support. He turned to ceramics, which had interested him since his childhood at *Takagamine*. Kenzan set up a kiln outside of Kyoto. There, one of his assistants was Seiemon, son of Ninsei, the most famous potter in Kyoto (see page 200). For about two years—around 1700—Korin joined in the activities of the kiln, coming out from Kyoto to paint designs on the flat rectangular dishes made by Kenzan. Using iron-oxide, Korin's soft brush moved freely over the white slip to compose the designs that were then fired and, finally, covered with a transparent glaze. This adaptation of a Chinese brush style on a smooth creamy-white, rectangular surface was a new idea in Japanese ceramics.

Attributed to Ogata Korin
"Yatsuhashi" Inkstone Box

Ogata Kenzan *Tray: Kyoto Ware*
Underglaze decoration by Korin

Kenzan and Korin *Dish with Design
of Plover Over Waves*

The two dishes reproduced here present motifs familiar in Korin's paintings—the iris and the wave. The iris dish is signed above the bridge by Korin, and signed on the back of the dish by Kenzan. A lively and even more sketchy effect is caught by Korin in that exhilarating wave breaking over the second dish. Above the wave, a flight of small, engaging *chidori* or plover are heading, it seems, straight into the wind. This brief but significant and creative enterprise echoes in a way the earlier collaboration between Koetsu and Sotatsu.

Kenzan is known to have had in his possession the personal notebooks of Koetsu and of Ninsei with their secret recipes for clays and glazes and firing techniques. It was at the Narutaki kiln that Kenzan probably made and decorated the set of round earthenware plates illustrated on page 219, so delightful in their informal and varied designs. The tea bowl on the next page with white flowers *(yugao)* and soft green leaves against a silver-gray ground demonstrates Kenzan's love of flowers, of the tea ceremony, and by allusion to a famous chapter, "Yugao," in *The Tale of Genji,* his love for the classical literature of Japan. The restraint of Zen taste and the charms of the decorative style seem to have been united in a single piece.

In 1731, at the age of sixty-eight, Kenzan was persuaded by a friend and patron to settle in Edo. There he began again composing paintings, poems, and ceramic pieces. Even at the age of eighty, Kenzan could paint a pair of handsome sixfold screens, *Hollyhocks and Plum Blossoms* (page 227) reminding us of the French painter Claude Monet, in his eighties, painting the water lilies of his own garden.

Ogata Kenzan *Tea Bowl with Flowers, "Yugao"*

Kenzan, painter, poet, and calligrapher, was probably more a designer of ceramics than a potter. He was not a master of wheel-throwing like Ninsei, the superb technician, whose enameled glazes recall the gorgeous lacquers and textiles of his time. But Kenzan's fluent brush, his perfect sense for suiting a design to the form of a pot, the immediacy and personal quality of everything he touched brought something new to ceramics in Japan. Kenzan died in poverty; but, in our own time, certain contemporary potters are considered so important that they are designated as "Living National Treasures" of Japan.

Ogata Kenzan *Hollyhocks and Plum Blossoms*

16
THE WINDS OF CHANGE

A passage from Hakluyt's *Voyages* (quoted at the beginning of Chapter 6) describes the unloading of goods from a Spanish ship returning from the Far East, captured by sailors of Queen Elizabeth, and brought into port on the English Channel in 1592. At about the same time, Japanese artists were painting descriptions of great Portuguese vessels unloading goods from India and China at the port of Nagasaki on the western end of Honshu Island. In the pair of screens illustrated, merchants are bringing ashore boxes and bales, porcelains, silks, and strange animals. They are greeted by a crowd of curious Japanese. A scattering of missionaries are among the more than 340 people represented on the two screens.

Artist Unknown
Namban Byobu (Southern Barbarians screens)

Namban Byobu (detail)

Foreigners whose vessels came from the south, blown by monsoon winds from India and from Canton, were called *Namban,* or "Southern Barbarians," by the Japanese. Portuguese merchants brought Indian cotton and Chinese silk to exchange for Japanese silver. Spanish vessels came in the 1590's, those of the Dutch and British around 1600, bringing with them telescopes, watches, and compasses, guns, playing cards, tobacco, and potatoes. Europeans in costumes of the period were almost as picturesque as the Japanese, and a source of great interest in Japan. Missionaries brought books with printed illustrations, and paintings, which were copied and adapted in Japan. The Western-style work, whether sacred or secular, was often the first experience in perspective and in modeling with light and shade for Japanese artists. This work in Western style together with Japanese-style paintings of foreigners on screens, porcelain, or lacquer is known as "Namban" art. Much of the Namban work was done by artists whose names are unknown to us today.

At first Western merchants and missionaries were welcomed in Japan. But the shogun came to fear their power. By 1614 the missionaries were expelled, and Japanese Christians were persecuted. In 1637 the Tokugawa government closed the doors of Japan to the outside world, admitting only an occasional Dutch ship to Nagasaki and restricting their crews to a tiny island in the harbor. The doors remained officially closed for the next two hundred years, but foreign goods were smuggled in, and inquiring Japanese studied the Dutch language in secret in order to understand something of Western science and invention. So in spite of official prohibition, a knowledge of Western styles of drawing and painting continued to filter into Japan. Later, some Western books with their illustrations were allowed to be imported. Eventually, European perspective and realism made themselves felt in the work of two artists we shall consider: Maruyama Okyo (1733–1795) and Katsushika Hokusai (1760–1849). But first we shall turn to a lively revival of interest in the painting of China, as seen in the art of Ikeno Taiga (1723–1776).

If the monsoon winds brought to Japan intimations of Europe by way of India, a fresh breeze in the second half of the seventeenth century also brought a new wave of Chinese influence. A few rather undistinguished Chinese painters settled in the Nagasaki region after the fall of the Ming dynasty. Their paintings of landscape, of birds and flowers, appealed to painters living in Kyoto who were bored by the conventional character of official painting. At the same time, illustrated handbooks showing the techniques of various Chinese masters began to circulate in Japan. The most famous of these manuals, *The Grain of Mustard Seed Garden,* was popular in Japan after about 1750. Published in a three-volume edition, it was the first work about Chinese art ever owned by this writer. Given to me long ago by a friend in Peking, the three volumes bound in blue cotton cloth have been loaned over the years to many

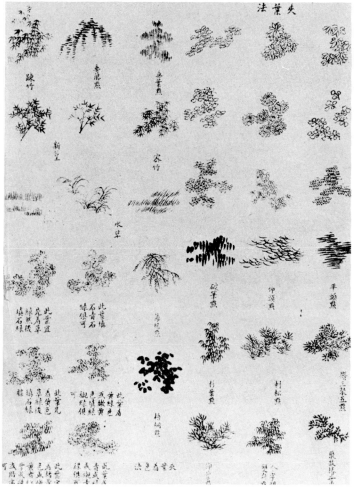

Brush Techniques for Foliage
from "The Grain of Mustard Seed Garden"

Landscape Page from
"The Grain of Mustard Seed Garden"

painters who have been intrigued by the patterns of foliage, the forms of rocks, the rhythms of water, by figures and landscape motifs. In these "quotations" from masters of the Chinese brush, much of the original subtlety was lost in the simplification and patternizing required by a woodcut print. This left the Japanese considerable freedom to invent their own variations on old-master themes.

Japanese artists working in what they thought was the manner of Chinese scholar-painters are described as belonging to the *Nanga* school. *Nanga* means southern painting and refers to the "Southern School" of Chinese art. *Nanga* is also called *Bunjinga,* or "Literary Men's Painting"—as many of the painters were also scholars or poets, or both. Creative, freewheeling, inventive in their borrowings from China, these artists somehow managed to remain intensely Japanese. They flourished with great distinction for about three generations, and the tradition continues to this day.

IKENO TAIGA *(1723–1776)*

One artist from the middle generation of the *Nanga* painters will have to stand, in this book, for the whole group. Ikeno Taiga, together with his friend Buson, a distinguished poet and painter, are generally considered the two most brilliant artists of the "Literary Men's School." Buson has already been introduced to readers of this book through his haiku poems in the chapter on Japan in "A Literary Interlude."

Suppose we look first at a hanging scroll by Ikeno Taiga to see what we can find out for ourselves. Painted with a lively and uninhibited brush, the patterns of foliage are sparkling, and as the detail shows, somewhat flat. Patterns that indicate rice paddies keep the same scale whether near or far. The mountain is set down in one swinging stroke, but given a sense of mass, like the foreground rocks, by a series of horizontal strokes

Ikeno Taiga *Fishing in Springtime*

Ikeno Taiga
Fishing in Springtime (detail)

in an allusion to the Chinese Sung dynasty painter, Mi Fei (1051–1107). One cannot look at the detail without sensing the sprightliness, the wit, and the apparent casualness of Ikeno Taiga's style. He seems to have been able to assimilate whatever he wished from the history of art. Like the scholar-painters of China he painted scrolls and album leaves, but he also worked on a large scale in ink and in color and gold on screens— something the Chinese scholar-artists would never have thought of doing.

Ikeno Taiga's father was a farmer who came to Kyoto to work at the mint, but who died when his son was only four years old. At five, the small boy was already admired for his calligraphy. At fourteen, he opened a fan shop and supported himself and his mother by painting from Chinese motifs. Taiga was from the beginning a professional painter, but his quick and eager mind made him many friends among scholars and

Ikeno Taiga *The Red Cliff*

Ikeno Taiga *Lan-t'ing*
(The Poetical Gathering at the Orchid Pavilion)

poets. That he was familiar with Chinese poetry may be assumed from his painting of the *Red Cliff* on page 233.[1] A screen more than twelve feet wide, now in a private collection in New York, illustrates Ikeno Taiga's work on a large scale. Like the painting of the *Red Cliff,* the subject of the painting *Lan-t'ing (The Poetical Gathering at the Orchid Pavilion)* is derived from Chinese literature. A group of scholars and poets have been sitting by the banks of a stream composing poetry and drinking wine from cups that go floating by. The gentleman at the writing table is probably the great calligrapher, Wang Hsi-chih, who wrote a poem about this elegant party in the year A.D. 353, complete with all the poems written by the forty-one friends who were present.

MARUYAMA OKYO *(1733–1795)*

Ikeno Taiga and the *Nanga* artists reacted in their own way against the stereotyped forms of official art under the Tokugawa government. Maruyama Okyo took a different route. Born into a farm family, and poor, Okyo had to make his own way. At seventeen he studied in Kyoto with a teacher of the Kano school, which meant training in the traditional ways of using the brush. He first came into contact with Western perspective and realism through seeing a peep show, perhaps in a toy shop where he worked as an assistant. Okyo actually made landscape designs of Japan, drawn in perspective, for this optical machine introduced by the Dutch. We know that Okyo admired certain old-master painters of China, that he knew well the Japanese Buddhist paintings in a monastery near Kyoto, and the decorative style of the Rimpa painters, the followers of Sotatsu and Korin.

None of these influences, however, was as important to Okyo as his own clear and direct observation of nature. He brought to the art of the eighteenth century what the Japanese call "a return to nature." Others had made fine sketches from nature, but none before him had made these direct and objective studies so central to their own work. Compare the brush drawing of a greyhound in gray ink by the German master, Albrecht Dürer (1471–1528) and the studies of a ferret done in ink and light color by Okyo on page 236. You will see how far truth to nature concerned them both. The *Ferret* is similar to a group of sketches that includes some rabbits and a marvelous duck, mounted on a hand scroll dated 1772, now in a private collection in Japan.

Look for a moment at three tigers on the following pages—with a cheer for the artists who made them. Alongside the mysterious tiger attributed to the Chinese artist Mu Ch'i, and the almost caricatured tiger of Sesshu's follower, Sesson, Okyo's animal may be described as realistic, less extraordinary than the earlier versions, and certainly easier to understand.

Albrecht Dürer
Greyhound German

Maruyama Okyo *Ferret*

Attributed to Mu Ch'i
Tiger

Sesson
Tiger and Dragon (detail)

Maruyama Okyo
Tiger in Wind and Rain

A screen called *Summer Night, Moonlight* on the next page achieves a wonderful effect of luminous, enveloping atmosphere. Here Okyo shows himself master of a special technique, the use of a broad flat brush held at an angle so that he could lay the paint on in tones from wet to dry, from dark to light, or from one color to another depending on the way the brush was "loaded." Known as the leading artist of Kyoto in the second half of the eighteenth century, Okyo received many commissions from great families for the screens that were his masterpieces.

Maruyama Okyo
Summer Night, Moonlight

Maruyama Okyo
Summer Night, Moonlight (detail)

KATSUSHIKA HOKUSAI (1760–1849)

The subject of Japanese woodcut prints has been of great interest in the West. Many books are available in English from 95-cent paperbacks and James Michener's substantial one-volume *Pictures of the Floating World* to the great catalogues of private collections that may be admired in our larger libraries. The reader is therefore encouraged to delve for himself into the fascinating story of printmakers and printmaking in Japan, a story that is beyond the scope of this book.

By the time of Hokusai, the techniques of the woodcut print in color, the methods of publishing and of distributing to an eager public, were already highly developed. This flourishing trade began in the Kyoto-Osaka region, but by Hokusai's time, Edo (modern Tokyo) was the center of immense activity in *Ukiyo-e,* or "Pictures of the Floating World." A title derived from a Buddhist term referring to the evanescence of life, it came to mean scenes of everyday life in the cities, the theatre, and the pleasure quarters. Pure landscape as a subject developed later, one of the creative innovations of Hokusai.

The adopted son of a mirror maker, learning the art of engraving as a boy, Hokusai was eighteen when he began cutting wood blocks for a well-known designer of actor prints, Shunsho. For a number of years the artist we know as Hokusai used the name Shunro, derived from his master's name. He was almost forty when he chose the "artist's name" by which he is generally known. In seventy years of continuous output, he used more than fifty names. Often they represented changes in his style or choice of subject matter. In later years Hokusai sometimes signed his work as *Gakyo Rojin,* translated as the "Old Man Mad about Painting," or the "Art-Crazy Old Man." Endowed with incredible vitality, restless, humorous, sometimes satirical, he was at the last a tragic figure. Hokusai died in poverty, still working at the age of ninety, having produced, it is said, some five hundred illustrated books and thirty thousand pictures.

In 1798, Hokusai designed a series of small prints, "Eight Views of Edo," inspired by Dutch engravings. Seen from a single low viewpoint, using an exaggerated one-point perspective, this approach to composition was unfamiliar to Japanese taste. Prints from the famous series *Thirty-six Views of Mount Fuji* show how this kind of borrowing from Europe was incorporated into designs for that masterful series of the 1820's. Two famous prints from the series are, *Fuji on a Clear Day with a Southerly Breeze,* popularly known as *The Red Fuji,* on page 240 and *The Great Wave,* on page 246.

Hokusai was a painter and a designer of prints; he was also a showman in a highly competitive, commercial world. Once Hokusai was summoned to appear before the shogun in a contest with Tani Buncho (1763–1840), the chief *Nanga* painter of his time in Edo. Hokusai first

Katsushika Hokusai *View from Nihon Bridge*

Katsushika Hokusai *Fuji on a Clear Day with a Southerly Breeze* painted a great curving river on a large paper screen. Then he splashed red paint on the feet of a cock and induced him to run over the blue river. Hokusai's painting recalled the old poem about maple leaves in autumn floating down the Tatsuta River. He was declared the winner.

In the same year as this contest—1804—Hokusai began drawing his *Fifty-three Stages Along the Tokaido,* the route from Edo to Kyoto. By 1814, he had begun publication, at the urging of loyal students, of his *Random Sketches* or *Sketches from Life,* known to us as the *Manga.* Thirteen volumes of these woodcut prints appeared in his lifetime, two more after his death. Townspeople and country people, their swift gestures and bustling activity, notes on plants, animals, birds, fishes, and insects, all are set down in a lively shorthand, the record of a lifetime of intense observation. Volumes from the *Manga* found their way to France after 1850 and were of absorbing interest to French painters and designers, a story to which we shall return.

Katsushika Hokusai *Page from the Manga, Nature Studies*

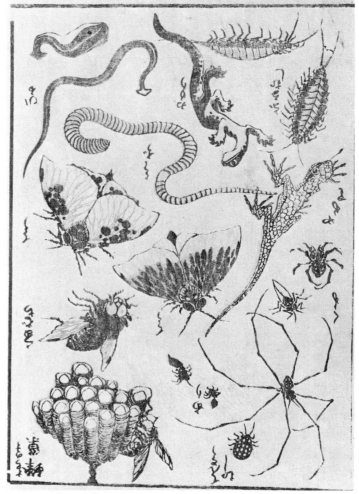

Katsushika Hokusai
Page from the Manga, Street People

Although Hokusai drew illustrations for hundreds of books and made many paintings, it is for his woodcut prints that he is chiefly honored. The prints may be divided into three main groups: landscapes, birds and flowers, and illustrations of Chinese and Japanese poetry. Among sets that he produced in the 1830's were *Waterfalls of Japan*, many fine bird and flower prints, and a new series, this time *One Hundred Views of Mount Fuji*, brought out in rivalry with Hiroshige, the popular artist of a new generation.

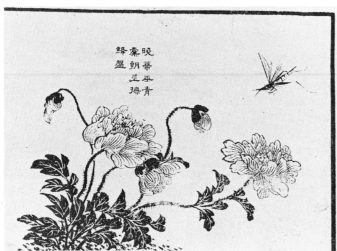

Page from "The Grain of Mustard Seed Garden," *Poppies*

Katsushika Hokusai
Oriental Poppies

A late series of prints, *The Imagery of the Poets of China and Japan*, brings us back to the subject of classical poetry. On the next page, the Chinese poet Li Po (*Ri Haku* in Japanese) is admiring the waterfall of Lu Shan. These are Li Po's lines:

> Sunlight streaming on Incense Stone
>   kindles a violet smoke;
> far off I watch the waterfall plunge
>   to the long river
> flying waters descending straight
>   three thousand feet
> till I think the Milky Way has
>   tumbled from the ninth height of Heaven.[2]

What Hokusai immediately conveys is the weight of water falling straight down "three thousand feet." In the boldness of his composition with its powerful rhythms, in the convoluted robes of the poet who seems as much a part of nature as rocks, trees, and waterfall, we sense both the originality and eccentricity that mark the work of Hokusai.

Katsushika Hokusai
Li Po Gazing at The Waterfall
of Lu-shan

JAPAN AND THE WEST: SOME NOTES

The winds of change that brought to Hokusai an awareness of European landscape traditions soon began to blow in the opposite direction—from Japan toward the Western world. Three years after Hokusai died, Commodore Perry appeared in Tokyo Bay with his "black ships"—black because of their smoke. Among the numerous gifts he brought ashore for the emperor were a miniature steam engine, one-quarter size, complete with track, tender, and car, two telegraph sets with three miles of wire, Audubon's *Birds of America* in nine volumes, a barrel of whiskey, and a box of champagne.[3] In Commodore Perry's published account of his expedition, there were some reproductions of Hokusai's prints. But the initial impact of Japanese woodcut prints in all their novelty and fascination for Western artists was felt, not in America, but in France. Through the establishment of commercial relations with Japan, art objects from the East began to appear in some quantity in Paris in the 1850's and 1860's. Japanese prints and curios were enthusiastically acquired by artists, collectors, and critics. For the next fifty years, what could be learned in Paris of the arts of Japan provided new sources of design, color, and composition for painters (Manet, Monet, Degas, Toulouse-Lautrec, among many others), for printmakers (a set was even produced called *The Thirty-six Views of the Eiffel Tower*), for designers of ceramics, of glass, like this vase, with its splendid carp derived from a page in the *Manga,* for designers of textiles, jewelry, and furniture. Sometimes the Japanese models were second-rate, and sometimes the artists were less than successful. But in the hands of the most creative of French artists their contact with the visual language of Japan provided a stimulus in a time that was ready for change. Mary Cassatt (1845–1926), working in Paris, and James McNeill Whistler (1834–1903), shuttling between Paris and London, were important American artists whose paintings and prints owe much to Japanese ideas. At the end of the nineteenth century and in the early twentieth, some of these underlying Japanese influences merged into the Art Nouveau style in the decorative arts. It is a style based on curvilinear forms derived from nature.

Once upon a beautiful June day in Tokyo, I went to visit the grounds of the Meiji Shrine, hoping to find the iris garden in full bloom. Along the bed of a small winding stream, between sloping green banks against a rich background of trees, poured a river of color—blue, purple, and white iris standing with their feet in water. Japanese visitors, quiet and appreciative, moved as if in a dream along either bank. They might have been looking at a long scroll unrolling, or at the endless panels of a painted screen. What I saw were the motifs, buds, blossoms, and slender leaves, that Korin translated into screens that are among his masterpieces. I saw also sunlight on the shallow golden-yellow muddy bottom from which the iris grew, exactly the effect of the gold ground in the

Eugene Rousseau *Glass Vase,* French

James McNeill Whistler
Caprice in Purple and Gold No. 2 American

screens by Korin's follower, Watanabe Shiko, screens that I knew by heart in the Cleveland Museum.

Not long after that visit to Japan, I stood in Monet's water-lily garden in Giverny on the Seine River in France. There were the water lilies, the great white clouds reflected in patches of open water, and at one end of the pond, completely overhung with wistaria, the little Japanese bridge. In Monet's house, a yellow dining room on the ground floor faced a garden bright with flowers, a room once hung with the painter's own collection of Japanese prints—figure compositions by Harunobu (1725–1770) and Utamaro (1753–1806), landscapes by Hokusai and Hiroshige, among others. In an old photograph[4] of the library, one can make out on the wall *The Red Fuji* and *The Great Wave* of Hokusai. Monet's friend, Debussy, chose *The Great Wave* as the cover for the first edition of the musical score of "La Mer" (1905).

Katsushika Hokusai
The Great Wave

Perhaps it is easier for us to observe the cultural exchanges of a hundred years ago than to see clearly those that may be going on in our own time. Japan seems to have accepted with eagerness Western technology and the influences of twentieth-century art. But it is not the Japanese prints or the decorated porcelains that influence Western craftsmen

Claude Monet *La Japonaise,* French (detail)

Yoshitushi
Japanese Girl in Western Dress (detail)

today. Rather it is the Zen taste, "tea taste," in ceramics: in the evidence of the hand's touch, the naturalness of the glaze, the understatement. Cultural exchanges have probably been most stimulating in architecture with Frank Lloyd Wright as a pioneer, bridging both worlds. Many aspects of Japanese architecture have been adapted to contemporary design in the West: modular units like the dimensions of tatami mats that determine the sizes of rooms; flexible use of space; the easy informal relations between interior and exterior space, between house and garden. Using modern building methods and materials yet keeping some of their inherited traditions, contemporary Japanese architects, working in all parts of the globe, have designed some of the finest modern buildings.

This infusion of culture from the East, although sometimes misunderstood and misused, continues to enrich the arts of the West, and through them the quality of our lives. An understanding of the traditional Japanese respect for nature, and delight in even its smallest forms, could lead us to a clearer recognition of human life as only one part of a greater whole. And now that the doors of China are reopening, we begin to feel the impact of a new Chinese culture. Who can dare to forecast what changes the winds aloft will bring to the East and the West in the next hundred years?

Postscript

After all this, how can you tell Chinese art from Japanese art? The answer is that you can't always tell. Scholars disagree about certain works made at times when Chinese influence was strongest in Japan. But there are some broad generalizations that can be made. Chinese painting is characteristically more philosophical, more reasoned, less given to extremes than Japanese painting. The Japanese are inclined to exaggeration, to extremes of statement, even to caricature. They have a flair for pattern and the decorative. In general, Japanese artists are more concerned with human situations, with individual types, with drama; Chinese painters with the harmony of man and nature, with poetry and philosophy. One might say that in architecture, city planning, and ceramics, the Chinese are liable to be concerned with

> symmetry
> scale
> formality.

The Japanese are more often concerned with

> asymmetry
> intimacy
> informality

In Japan, what we sometimes designate as the fine arts have always kept close touch with the crafts—in fact the distinction hardly exists in Japan. As we have seen, many of their great artists at times have turned their skills to decorative screens, to designing for textiles, or ceramics, or wood-block prints. This is not the case in China, where a distinction has traditionally existed between the gentlemen-scholar artists, the *literati,* and the more anonymous artisan painters, the craftsmen in ceramics, and the sculptors.

Taoism in China, Shinto in Japan, provided a grounding in the intuitive relation of men to the world of nature around them, to the inherent character of materials—wood, stone, clay, paper, and ink. The Buddhism that spread from India to China, and later to Japan, brought at one extreme a formal, "high church" religion, an elaborate theology, a colorful ritual and ceremony. At the opposite extreme, Ch'an Buddhism in China, Zen in Japan, provided an understated, an astringent, a paradoxical note in the arts.

The world of Chinese culture, already ancient at the time of the coming of Buddhism, was the classical background of Japan, source of the written language, of much in government and in the literary tradition, just as the Mediterranean culture of Greece and Rome stands behind the modern Western world. Like the revival of interest in the antique at the beginning of the Renaissance, there have been, in Japan, periods of a revival of interest in the Chinese tradition. But one should not be beguiled by parallels. The differences between developments in the East and in the West are enormous, as they are between the most characteristic arts of China and of Japan.

It is the comparisons and contrasts that are endlessly intriguing. Delight in the small, the endearing, the enchanting, and awe at the splendid, the lofty, the mysterious—these are some of the rewards for venturing within the Eastern Gate.

Notes

TO THE READER

1. Ezra Pound, trans., *Shih-Ching: the Classic Anthology Defined by Confucius* (Cambridge: Harvard University Press, 1954), p. 44. Copyright © 1954 by the President and Fellows of Harvard College.

CHAPTER 1

1. Arthur Waley, trans., *One Hundred and Seventy Poems* (London: Constable and Company, Ltd., 1918), p. 151. Copyright © 1919 and renewed 1947 by Arthur Waley. Reprinted by permission of Constable and Company, Ltd., and Alfred A. Knopf, Inc.

CHAPTER 2

1. Gia-fu Feng and Jane English, trans., *Lao Tsu: Tao Te Ching* (New York: Alfred A. Knopf, Inc.), Copyright © 1972 by Gia-fu Feng and Jane English. Reprinted by permission of Alfred A. Knopf, Inc.

2. Gary Snyder, trans., *Cold Mountain Poems* (*Evergreen Review*, II, 6), Autumn, 1958.

3. Arthur F. Wright, *Buddhism in Chinese History* (Stanford, California: Stanford University Press, 1959), p. 79.

CHAPTER 3

1. Wytter Bynner, trans., from the texts of Kiang Kang-hu, *The Jade Mountain: A Chinese Anthology* (New York: Vintage Books, Random House, 1972), p. 33. Copyright © 1929 and renewed 1957 by Alfred A. Knopf, Inc. Reprinted by permission of the publisher.

CHAPTER 4

1. Osvald Sirèn, ed. and trans., *The Chinese on the Art of Painting* (New York: Schocken Books, Inc., 1963), p. 234. Copyright © 1963 by Schocken Books, Inc. Reprinted by permission of the publisher and Hong Kong University Press, Hong Kong.

2. Hugh Honour in *Arts of China* by editors of Horizon Magazine (New York: American Heritage Publishing Company, Inc., 1969), p. 32.

3. Shio Sakanishi, trans., *An Essay on Landscape Painting by Kuo Hsi* (London: John Murray Ltd., 1935), p. 31.

4. Wai-kam Ho, *Li Ch'eng and the Mainstream of Northern Sung Painting* (proceedings of the International Symposium on Chinese Painting, Taipei: National Palace Museum, 1970), pp. 251–283.

5. James Cahill, *Treasures of Asia—Chinese Painting* (Lausanne: Skira, 1960), p. 80.

6. Hugo Munsterberg, *The Collection of Chinese Paintings in the Cincinnati Art Museum* (Detroit: *The Art Quarterly*, Vol XV, 1952), p. 308.

7. Sherman E. Lee, *Ma Yuan* (Encyclopedia of World Art (New York: McGraw Hill, 1964).

8. Susan Bush, *The Chinese Literati on Painting: Su Shih (1037–1101) to Tung Ch'i Ch'ang (1555–1636)* (Cambridge, Massachusetts: Harvard University Press, 1971), p. 139.

9. C. T. Li, *The Freer Sheep and Goat and Chao Meng-fu's Horse Paintings* (Ascona, Switzerland: Artibus Asiae, Vol 30, 1968), p. 281.

10. Richard Edwards, *The Field of Stones, A Study of the Art of Shen Chou (1427–1509)* (Washington: Smithsonian Institution, Freer Gallery of Art, Oriental Studies, No. 5, 1962), p. 40. *The Return from Stone Lake* is now in the Art Institute of Chicago.

11. ———, *The Field of Stones*, p. 40.

12. Marilyn and Shen Fu, *Studies in Connoisseurship, Chinese Paintings from the Arthur M. Sackler Collection* (Princeton University: The Art Museum, 1973), p. 55.

13. Osvald Sirèn, *The Chinese on the Art of Painting*, p. 187.

14. Sherman E. Lee, *Chinese Landscape Painting* (The Cleveland Museum of Art, distributed by Harry N. Abrams, Inc., New York: 1962) 2nd edition, p. 148.

15. Lin Yutang, trans., *The Chinese Theory of Art* (London: William Heinemann, Ltd., 1967), p. 148. Copyright © 1976 by Dr. Lin Yutang. Reprinted by permission of G. P. Putnam's Sons.

CHAPTER 5

1. T. S. Eliot, from "Burnt Norton" in the "Four Quartets," from *Collected Poems 1909–1962* (New York: Harcourt, Brace and World, Inc., 1963), p. 180.

2. Soame Jenyns, *Ming Pottery and Porcelain* (London: Faber and Faber), p. 121.

3. William B. Honey, *The Ceramic Art of China and Other Countries of the Far East* (London: Faber and Faber, and Hyperion Press, Ltd., 1945), p. 19.

4. Lady David, *Ch'ing Enamelled Wares in the Percival David Foundation of Chinese Art* (University of London: School of Oriental and African Studies, 1958), p. 33.

CHAPTER 6

1. Richard Hakluyt, *Voyages*, (London: J. M. Dent, 1927), Vol. V, p. 66.

2. James Merrill, *Braving the Elements* (New York: Atheneum, 1972), pp. 36, 37. Copyright © 1969, 1972 by James Merrill. Reprinted by permission of Atheneum Publishers.

3. Nora Waln, *The House of Exile* (Boston: Little, Brown and Co., 1933), p. 3. Copyright © 1933 by Little, Brown and Co.

CHAPTER 7

1. *Illustrated London News,* September, 1976.

2. Barbara W. Tuchman, *Notes From China* (New York: Collier Books, 1972), p. 47. Copyright © 1972 by The Associated Press. Copyright © 1972 by Barbara W. Tuchman.

CHAPTER 8

1. S. H. Chen, trans., *Lu Chi: Essay on Literature* (Portland, Maine: Anthoensen Press, 1953), p. 214.

2. John Milton, *Paradise Lost*, Book IV, lines 323–327.

3. Arthur Waley, trans., *The Book of Songs* (New York: Grove Press, Inc., Evergreen Edition, 1960, distributed by Random House). First published in 1937 by George Allen and Unwin Ltd., p. 30. Reprinted by permission of Grove Press, Inc.

4. Helen Waddell, trans., *Lyrics from the Chinese* (London: Constable and Company, 1921) p. 39. First published in 1913.

5. Ezra Pound, trans., *Shih-Ching: The Classic Anthology Defined by Confucius*, (Cambridge: Massachusetts, Harvard University Press, 1954), p. 208, 209.

6. David Hawkes, trans. *Ch'u Tz'u, The Songs of the South, An Ancient Chinese Anthology* (Oxford: Oxford University Press, 1959), pp. 105, 106. Copyright © 1959 by Oxford University Press. Reprinted by permission of Oxford University Press.

7. Arthur Waley, trans. *Nine Songs, A Study of Shamanism in Ancient China* (San Francisco: City of Lights Books, 1973), p. 47. First published by George Allen and Unwin, Ltd., 1955.

8. David Hawkes, trans. *Ch'u Tz'u, The Songs of the South*, p. 44.

9. William Acker, *T'ao the Hermit, Sixty Poems by T'ao Ch'ien* (London and New York: Thames and Hudson, 1952), p. 53.

10. Cyril Birch, ed. and trans., *Anthology of Chinese Literature* (New York: Grove Press, Inc., 1965) p. 167. Copyright © 1965 by Grove Press, Inc. Reprinted by permission of Grove Press, Inc.

11. C. H. Kwock and Vincent McHugh, trans. Quoted in Cyril Birch, *Anthology of Chinese Literature*, pp. 225–226.

12. *Ibid.*

13. Witter Bynner and Kiang Kang-hu, *The Jade Mountain*, p. 170.

14. Kenneth Rexroth, *One Hundred Poems from the Chinese* (New York: New Directions, 1956), p. 26. Copyright © 1971 by Kenneth Rexroth. All rights reserved. Reprinted by permission of New Directions Publishing Corporation.

15. Cyril Birch, ed. and trans., *An Anthology of Chinese Literature*, p. 238.

16. Michael Sullivan, *Chinese Art, Recent Discoveries* (London and New York: Thames and Hudson, 1973), p. 24.

17. Arthur Waley, *One Hundred and Seventy Chinese Poems*, p. 144.

18. *Ibid.*, p. 149.

19. ———, *Chinese Poems* selected from *170 Chinese Poems, More Translations from the Chinese, The Temple*, and the *Book of Songs* (London: George Allen and Unwin, Ltd., 1946), pp. 142, 143.

20. A. C. Graham, trans. in Birch: *Anthology of Chinese Literature*, p. 368.

21. Burton Watson, trans., *Introduction to Sung Poetry by Kojiro Yoshikawa* (Cambridge: Harvard University Press, 1967), p. 122.

22. A. C. Graham, trans., in Birch: *Anthology of Chinese Literature*, pp. 381, 382.

23. S. H. Chen, trans., Lu Chi: *Essay on Literature*, p. 207.

CHAPTER 9

1. Donald Keene, trans., *Essays in Idleness*, "The Tsurezuregusa of Kenko" (New York and London: Columbia University Press, 1967), p. 12. Reprinted by permission of Columbia University Press.

2. *The Manyoshu*, The Nippon Gakujutsu Shinkokai Translation of One Thousand Poems, foreword by Donald Keene (New York and London: Columbia University Press, 1965), Unesco Collection of Representative Works, Japanese Series, p. 3. Reprinted by permission of Columbia University Press.

3. *Ibid.*, p. 134.

4. Kenneth Rexroth, *One Hundred Poems from the Japanese* (New York: New Directions, 1964), p. 66. All rights reserved. Reprinted by permission of New Directions Publishing Corporation.

5. *The Manyoshu*, p. 138.

6. *Ibid.*, pp. 46–47.

7. Arthur Waley, trans., *Japanese Poetry, The Uta* (London: Percy Lund, Humphries and Company, Ltd., 1959), p. 58.

8. *Ibid.*, p. 66.

9. *Ibid.*, p. 67.

10. Kenneth Rexroth, *One Hundred Poems from the Japanese*, p. 36.

11. Donald Keene, ed., *Anthology of Japanese Literature, From the Earliest Era to*

the Mid-Nineteenth Century (New York: Grove Press, Inc., 1955), p. 194. Copyright © 1955 by Grove Press, Inc. Reprinted by permission of Donald Keene and Grove Press, Inc.

12. *Ibid.*, p. 196.

13. Donald Keene, *Landscapes and Portraits, Appreciations of Japanese Culture* (Tokyo and Palo Alto: Kodansha International, Ltd., 1973), p. 17.

14. Helen Craig McCullough, trans., *Tales of Ise, Lyrical Episodes from Tenth-Century Japan* (Stanford, Calif.: Stanford University Press, 1968), p. 75.

15. Edward Seidensticker, trans., *Murasaki Shikibu, The Tale of Genji* (New York: Alfred A. Knopf, 1976), Vol. 1, p. 132.

16. *Ibid,* p. 237.

17. Ivan Morris, trans. and ed., *The Pillow Book of Sei Shonagon* (New York: Columbia University Press, 1967), Vol. 1, p. 1. Reprinted by permission of Columbia University Press and Oxford University Press.

18. *Ibid,* Vol. 1, p. 33.

19. *Ibid,* Vol. 1, p. 90.

20. *Ibid,* Vol. 1, p. 268.

21. Donald Keene, ed., *Anthology of Japanese Literature,* pp. 258, 259.

22. Donald Keene, *Japanese Literature, An Introduction for Western Readers* (New York: Grove Press, Inc., 1955), pp. 39 and 40. Copyright © 1955 by Donald Keene. Reprinted by permission of Georges Borchardt, Inc., 136 East 57th Street, N.Y., N.Y.

23. *Ibid,* p. 39.

24. *Ibid,* p. 40.

25. Harold G. Henderson, *The Bamboo Broom, An Introduction to Japanese Haiku* (Boston and New York: Houghton Mifflin Company, 1934), p. 37. Reprinted by permission of Mrs. Harold G. Henderson.

26. *Ibid,* p. 41.

27. Noboyuki Yuasa, trans., *The Narrow Road to the Deep North and Other Travel Sketches* (Harmondsworth, Middlesex, England: Pelican Classics, 1966), pp. 97, 98. Copyright © 1966 by Noboyuki Yuasa. Reprinted by permission of Penguin Books, Inc.

28. *Ibid,* pp. 115, 116.

29. Harold G. Henderson, *An Introduction to Haiku, An Anthology of Poems and Poets from Basho to Shiki* (Garden City, N.Y.: Doubleday and Company, Doubleday Anchor Books, 1955), p. 105. Reprinted by permission of Mrs. Harold G. Henderson.

30. *Ibid,* p. 104.

31. *Ibid,* p. 112.

32. D. T. Suzuki, *Zen and Japanese Culture* (London: Routledge and Kegan Paul, 1950), p. 383.

CHAPTER 10

1. Kenneth Rexroth, *One Hundred Poems from the Japanese,* p. 60.

CHAPTER 11

1. Sir George Sansom, *A History of Japan* (Stanford, Calif.: Stanford University Press, 1958–1963, 3 vols.), Vol. 1, p. 63.

CHAPTER 12

1. Shingon is a sect of Esoteric Buddhism. Esoteric means "intended for or understood by only a few."

2. Ryusaku Tsunoda, Wm. Theodore de Bary, and Donald Keene, comps., *Sources of the Japanese Tradition* (New York: Columbia University Press, 1958), Vol. 1, p. 137.

3. Robert Treat Paine and Alexander Soper, *The Art and Architecture of Japan* (Baltimore: Penguin Books, 1955), p. 214.

4. Edward C. Seidensticker, trans., *The Tale of Genji,* Vol. 1, p. 407.

5. Ivan Morris, trans. *The Pillow Book of Sei Shonagon,* Vol. 1, p. 234.

6. Edward C. Seidensticker, trans. *The Tale of Genji*, Vol. 2, p. 669.

7. *Ibid*, Vol. 1, p. 519.

CHAPTER 13

1. Edward C. Seidensticker, trans. *The Tale of Genji*, Vol. 2, p. 761.

2. Yoshinobu Tokugawa, in the introduction to Ivan Morris, *The Tale of Genji Scroll* (Tokyo: Kodansha International, 1977), p. 9.

3. Adapted from a translation of the story written on the scroll.

4. Robert Hughes and Donald Richie, eds., *Rashomon, a Film by Akira Kurosawa* (New York: Grove Press, 1952), p. 7. Reprinted by permission of Robert P. Mills, Ltd.

CHAPTER 14

1. Wai-kam Ho, *Kao; Myth and Speculations* (Cleveland Museum of Art Bulletin, Vol. 50, No. 4, April, 1963), p. 74.

2. Jon Covell and Abbot Sobin Yamada, *Zen at Daitoku-ji* (Tokyo: Kodansha International, 1974), p. 186.

3. Otto Benesch, *Rembrandt as a Draughtsman* (New York: Phaidon Publishers, 1960), p. 29. *Pentimenti* are the tentative statements, the repentances or corrections, of an artist in a drawing or a painting.

4. *Ibid*, p. 30.

5. Yukio Yashiro, *2000 Years of Japanese Art* (London: Thames and Hudson, 1958), p. 22.

6. Jon Carter Covell, *Under the Seal of Sesshu* (New York: De Pamphilis Press, Inc., 1941), p. 11.

7. Fujio Koyama, *Japanese Ceramics from Ancient to Modern Times* (Oakland: Oakland Art Museum, 1961), p. 27.

CHAPTER 15

1. Sir George B. Sansom, *Japan, A Short Cultural History* (New York: Century Company, 1931), p. 429.

2. Helen C. McCullough, trans. *Tales of Ise*, p. 115.

3. Hiroshi Mizuo, *Edo Painting: Sotatsu and Korin*, trans. by John N. Shields (New York and Tokyo: Weatherhill/Heibonsha, 1972), p. 105.

4. Sherman E. Lee, *Japanese Decorative Style* (The Cleveland Museum of Art, distributed by Harry N. Abrams, 1961), p. 80.

5. Helen C. McCullough, trans. *Tales of Ise*, p. 75.

CHAPTER 16

1. For "The Red Cliff," *see* Chapter 8, "China, A Literary Interlude," p. 129.

2. Burton Watson, *Chinese Lyricism, Shih Poetry from the Second to the Twelfth Century, with translations* (New York: Columbia University Press, 1971), p. 146.

3. Roger Pineau, ed., *The Japan Expedition, 1853–1854; The Personal Journal of Commodore Mathew C. Perry* (Washington, D.C.: Smithsonian Institution, 1968), p. 233.

4. Claire Joyes, *Monet at Giverny*, (London: Mathews, Miller Dunbar, 1975), p. 72.

List of Illustrations

hand scroll *Barbarian Royalty Worshipping Buddha,* attributed to the painter Chao Kuang-fu (Northern Sung dynasty). Ink on paper. H. 26.8 cm (10⁹/₁₆″). The Cleveland Museum of Art, Mr. and Mrs. Severance A. Millikin Collection, **43 left**

Ch'en Shun (1483–1544), Ming dynasty. Inscription of the essay by Chung Ch'ang-t'ung (179–219), *A Reasoning on Ideal Happiness,* dated 1539. Detail of a hand scroll, ink on paper. H. 34.5, L. 666.7 cm (13½″ × 262½″). Honolulu Academy of Arts, Given by Friends in Memory of Mrs. A. E. Steadman, 1960, **43 below right**

CHAPTER 4   A CHOICE OF ARTISTS

Artist unknown (Chinese, T'ang dynasty). *The Emperor Ming Huang's Journey to Shu.* Hanging scroll, ink and color on silk. H. 55.9 cm (21³/₄″). Collection of the National Palace Museum, Taipei, Taiwan, Republic of China, **49**

Attributed to Li Ch'eng (active 940–967). *Buddhist Temple Amid Clearing Mountain Peaks,* Northern Sung dynasty. Hanging scroll, ink and color on silk. H. 111.8, W. 55.9 cm (44″ × 22″). Nelson Gallery-Atkins Museum, Kansas City, Missouri (Nelson Fund), **66**

Detail from *Buddhist Temple Amid Clearing Mountain Peaks,* attributed to Li Ch'eng, **50**

Ma Yuan (active 1190–1225), Southern Sung dynasty. *On a Mountain Path in Spring.* Album leaf, ink and color on silk. H. 27.4 cm (10³/₄″). Collection of the National Palace Museum, Taipei, Taiwan, Republic of China, **52**

Ma Yuan (active 1190–1225), Southern Sung dynasty. *The Four Sages of Shang Shan.* Hand scroll, ink and color on paper. H. 33.6, L. 307 cm (13¼″ × 121″). The Cincinnati Art Museum, Anonymous Gift, **54**

Chao Meng-fu (1254–1322), Yuan dynasty. *Bamboos, Rocks and Lonely Orchids.* Hand scroll, ink on paper. H. 50.5, L. 144.2 cm (19⁷/₈″ × 56³/₄″). The Cleveland Museum of Art, Purchase, John L. Severance Fund, **57 above**

Detail of Chao Meng-fu's *Bamboos, Rocks and Lonely Orchids,* **57 below**

Chao Meng-fu (1254–1322), Yuan dynasty. *Sheep and Goat.* Hand scroll, ink on paper. H. 25.2, L. 48.4 cm (9¹⁵/₁₆″ × 19¹/₁₆″). Courtesy of the Smithsonian Institution, Freer Gallery of Art, Washington, D.C., **58**

Detail of Chao Meng-fu's *Sheep and Goat,* **67 above**

Jen Jen-fa (1254–1327), Yuan dynasty. *Three Horses and Four Grooms.* Hand scroll, ink and color on silk. H. 29.3, L. 136.9 cm (11½″ × 53⁷/₈″). The Cleveland Museum of Art, Purchase, Leonard C. Hanna, Jr. Bequest, **66 and 67 below**

Shen Chou (1427–1509), Ming dynasty. *Man, Bird and Boy in a Boat.* One of six album leaves mounted as a hand scroll (5 leaves by Shen Chou, 1 leaf by Wen Cheng-ming), ink and color on paper. H. 38.7, W. 60.3 cm (15¼″ × 23³/₄″). Nelson Gallery-Atkins Museum, Kansas City, Missouri (Nelson Fund), **61 above**

Shen Chou (1427–1509), Ming dynasty. *The Sword Spring.* Leaf from the album *Twelve Views of Tiger Hill, Suchou,* ink on paper. H. 31.1, L. 40.2 cm (12¹/₄″ × 15¹³/₁₆″). The Cleveland Museum of Art, Leonard C. Hanna, Jr., Bequest, **61 below**

Tao-Chi (1641–after 1704), Ch'ing dynasty. *Ten Thousand Ugly Ink Blots.* Hand scroll, ink on paper. Detail. H. 25.6, L. 227 cm (10¹/₄″ × 89³/₈″). Su-chou Museum, **63**

Tao-Chi (1641–after 1704), Ch'ing dynasty. *Spring on the Min River,* 1697.

Hanging scroll, ink and color on paper. H. 39, L. 52 cm (15³/₈″ × 20⁷/₁₆″). The Cleveland Museum of Art, Purchase, John L. Severance Fund, **64 above**

Detail of Tao-Chi's *Spring on the Min River,* **64 below**

Tao-Chi (1641–after 1704), Ch'ing dynasty. *Study in Wet Ink, (Waterside Hut).* One of twelve album leaves in ink and colors on paper. H. 24.1, W. 28 cm (9¹/₂″ × 11″). Collection of C. C. Wang, **65**

CHAPTER 5   THE CERAMIC TRADITION

Saucer: Ting Ware. China. 13th–14th century. Glazed porcelain. Diam. 12.7 cm (5″). Courtesy, The Percival David Foundation of Chinese Art, London, **70 above**

Preparing for the Lotus Lantern Dance. Photograph taken by the author in Ting Hsien, Hopei, **70 below**

Vase: Pan-shan type, from Kansu Province. China. Neolithic period. Earthenware. H. 36.2 cm (14¹/₄″). The Cleveland Museum of Art, Purchase, The Charles W. Harkness Endowment Fund, **72 top left**

Jar. China. Shang dynasty, late 13th–early 12th century B.C. Earthenware. H. 33.2, Diam. 28.3 cm (13¹/₁₆″ × 11¹/₈″). Courtesy of the Smithsonian Institution, Freer Gallery of Art, Washington, D.C., **72 top right**

House Model. China. Han dynasty, 206 B.C.–A.D. 221. Polychromed earthenware. H. 132.1, D. 68.6, W. 85.1 cm (52″ × 27″ × 33¹/₂″). Nelson Gallery-Atkins Museum, Kansas City, Missouri (Nelson Fund), **72 below**

Horse. China. T'ang dynasty. Earthenware with polychrome glaze. H. 76.9, L. 80.3 cm (30¹/₄″ × 31⁵/₈″). The Cleveland Museum of Art, Anonymous Gift, **72 and 86 above**

Ewer with Phoenix-headed Spout: Chi-chou Ware. China. Late T'ang dynasty. Glazed porcelain. H. 34.3 cm (15³/₈″). Reproduced by courtesy of the Trustees of the British Museum, **74 right**

Bowl: Yueh Ware. China. Five Dynasties, 10th century. Glazed stoneware. Diam. 27 cm (10⁵/₈″). The Metropolitan Museum of Art, Rogers Fund, 1917, **74 left**

Conical Bowl: Ting Ware. China. Northern Sung dynasty, 12th century. Glazed porcelain. Diam. 20.3 cm (8″). The Cleveland Museum of Art, Purchase, Dudley P. Allen Fund, **75 left**

Vase: Tz'u-chou Ware. China. Northern Sung dynasty, 12th century. Stoneware with underglaze slip coatings. H. 34.3 cm (13¹/₂″). The Cleveland Museum of Art, J. H. Wade Collection, **75 right**

Vase with Handles of Fish Form: Lung-ch'uan Ware. China. Sung dynasty. Glazed porcelain. H. 25.9, Diam. 11.3 cm (10³/₁₆″ × 4⁷/₁₆″). Courtesy of the Smithsonian Institution, Freer Gallery of Art, Washington, D.C., **76 top**

Incense Burner: Kuan Ware. China. Southern Sung dynasty. Glazed porcelain. W. 15.6 cm (6¹/₈″). The Cleveland Museum of Art, Mr. and Mrs. Severance A. Millikin Collection, **76 bottom**

Tea Bowl: Ch'ien Ware. China. Sung dynasty. Glazed stoneware. H. 7, Diam. 12.4 cm (2³/₄″ × 4⁷/₈″). The Cleveland Museum of Art, The Fanny Tewksbury King Collection, **77 top**

Covered Vase. China. Yuan dynasty, second half of the 14th century. Porcelain decorated in underglaze blue. H. 38 cm (14¹⁵/₁₆″). Courtesy, Museum of Fine Arts, Boston, **77 bottom**

Large Dish. China. Ming dynasty, early 15th century. Porcelain with underglaze blue decoration. H. 9.5, Diam. 68 cm (3³/₄″ × 26³/₄″). Courtesy of the Smithsonian Institution, Freer Gallery of Art, Washington, D.C., **78 left**

Vase: Fa-hua type. China. Ming dynasty, late 15th century. Glazed stoneware. H. 37.5 cm (14³/₄"). The Cleveland Museum of Art, John L. Severance Collection, **78 right**

Wine Cup. China. Ming dynasty, mark and reign of Ch'eng Hua (1465–1487). Porcelain with underglaze blue and overglaze red and green enamels. H. 4.8 cm (1⁷/₈"). The Cleveland Museum of Art, Purchase, John L. Severance Fund, **79 right margin**

Bowl for Goldfish. China. Ch'ing dynasty, reign of K'ang Hsi (1662–1722). Porcelain with *famille verte* decoration. H. 29.2, Diam. 55 cm (11¹/₂" × 21⁵/₈"). Nelson Gallery-Atkins Museum, Kansas City, Missouri (Nelson Fund), **79 middle**

Flying Horse Later Han dynasty
Library Table. China. Ming dynasty, 16th century. Huang-hua-li wood. *Side Chairs,* China. Ming dynasty, 16th century. Huang-hua-li wood (Lent by Elizabeth Hay Bechtel). *Scroll' Garden Rock,* by Tso Chen, c. 1700. Bowl for goldfish (see above). Nelson Gallery-Atkins Museum, Kansas City, Missouri (Nelson Fund), **79 below**

Pilgrim Vase: Lang Ware. China. Ch'ing dynasty, reign of K'ang Hsi (1662–1722). Porcelain with oxblood red glaze. H. 22.5 cm (8⁷/₈"). The Cleveland Museum of Art, Bequest of John L. Severance, **80 left**

Vase of Ch'ien-lung Enameled Porcelain. China. Ch'ing dynasty, mark and reign of Ch'ien Lung (1736–1795). Glazed porcelain with *famille rose* decoration. H. 20.3 cm (8"). Courtesy, The Percival David Foundation of Chinese Art, London, **80 right**

CHAPTER 6   THE BRIDGE ON THE WILLOW PLATE

Giovanni Bellini (c. 1430–1516). *The Feast of the Gods.* Painting, oil on canvas. H. 170, W. 188 cm (67" × 74"). Photograph, Courtesy of the National Gallery of Art, Washington, D.C., Widener Collection, **82 (detail), 270**

Medici Plate. Italy. Florentine, c. 1580. Soft-paste porcelain. Diam. 28 cm (11"). The Cleveland Museum of Art, Purchase, The John L. Severance Fund, **83**

Abraham van Beyeren (1620/21–1690). *Still Life with a Silver Wine Jar and a Reflected Portrait of the Artist.* Painting, oil on canvas. H. 99.7, W. 82.5 cm (39¹/₄" × 32¹/₂"). The Cleveland Museum of Art, Purchase, Mr. and Mrs. William H. Marlatt Fund, **85**

Höchst Group: Chinese Emperor. Germany, c. 1770, made by Johann Peter Melchior (1742–1825). Glazed porcelain. H. 37.5 cm (15⁷/₈"). The Metropolitan Museum of Art, Gift of R. Thornton Wilson, 1950, in Memory of Florence Ellsworth Wilson, **84**

Porcelain Plate. France, painted by Dieu, 1792. Sèvres blackware. Diam. 24.8 cm (9³/₄"). Nelson Gallery-Atkins Museum, Kansas City, Missouri, Gift of Arnold Seligmann, Rey and Co., **89**

Canton Mug and Plate. Chinese export porcelain, c. 1810. Diam. of plate 25.5 cm (10¹/₁₆"). H. of mug 11 cm (4³/₈"). Privately owned. Photograph by Martin Linsey, **88 left**

Willow Plate. England, 19th century. Glazed earthenware. Diam. 25 cm (10"). Privately owned. Photograph by the author, **88 right**

Attributed to Lam Qua, Ch'ing dynasty. *Houqua,* c. 1830. Oil on canvas. H. 76.2, W. 63.5 cm (30" × 25"). Museum of the American China Trade, Milton, Massachusetts, **91**

Extension Chair. China, c. 1810. Bamboo and cane. L. 102.9 cm (40¹/₂") when

Detail, *Head of Attendant of the Princess Yung-t'ai.* Photograph after *T'ang Yung-t'ai kung-chu mu-pi-hua chi,* Peking, 1963, **101 right**

Archaeologists Measuring Pottery Warriors from the Tomb of Ch'in Shih Huang-ti. China. Ch'in dynasty, c. 210 B.C. Earthenware. Excavated at Lin-t'ung, Shensi Province. Photograph after *China Pictorial,* 1975, no. 11, **103 above**

A Corner of the Pit Where Horses and Warriors Were Excavated. China. Ch'in dynasty, c. 210 B.C. From the tomb of Ch'in Shih Huang-ti at Lin-t'ung, Shensi Province. Photograph after *China Pictorial,* 1975, no. 11, **103 below**

Warrior Figure (restored). China. Ch'in dynasty, c. 210 B.C. Earthenware. Excavated from the tomb of Ch'in Shih Huang-ti at Lin-t'ung, Shensi Province. H. 182 cm (71⅝"). Photograph after *China Pictorial,* 1975, no. 11, **104 right**

Head of Warrior. Excavated from the tomb of Ch'in Shih Huang-ti. Photograph after *Wen Wu,* 1975, no. 11, **104 left**

CHAPTER 8   A LITERARY INTERLUDE: CHINA

Shen Chou (1427–1509), Ming dynasty. *Poet on a Mountain.* One of six album leaves mounted as a hand scroll (5 leaves by Shen Chou, 1 leaf by Wen Cheng-ming), ink and color on paper. H. 38.7, W. 60.3 cm (15¼" × 23¾"). Nelson Gallery-Atkins Museum, Kansas City, Missouri (Nelson Fund), **110**

Chang Wu (active 1335–1365), Yuan dynasty. *Imaginary Portrait of Ch'u Yuan,* section from the hand scroll *The Nine Songs,* dated 1360. Ink on paper. H. 28, L. 438.2 cm (28" × 172½"). The Cleveland Museum of Art, Purchase from the J. H. Wade Fund, **116**

Chang Wu (active 1335–1365). *Riding on a White Turtle* from *The Nine Songs* hand scroll, **117 above**

Ch'en Hung-shou (1599–1652), Ming dynasty. *Imaginary Portrait of T'ao Ch'ien.* Detail from the hand scroll, *Episodes in the Life of T'ao Ch'ien,* dated 1650. Ink and color on silk. H. 30.5, L. 302.5 cm (12" × 121"). Honolulu Academy of Arts, Purchase, 1954, **117 below**

Yao T'ing-mei (active 14th century), Yuan dynasty. *Leisure Enough to Spare.* Detail from a hand scroll, ink on paper. H. 23, L. 84 cm (9 1/16" × 33 1/16"). The Cleveland Museum of Art, Purchase, John L. Severance Fund, **118**

Tao-Chi (1641–after 1704), Ch'ing dynasty. *The Peach-blossom Spring,* after the story by T'ao Ch'ien. Hand scroll, ink and color on paper. H. 25, L. 157.8 cm (9⅞" × 62¼"). Courtesy of the Smithsonian Institution, Freer Gallery of Art, Washington, D.C., **120 and 121**

Hua Yen (1682–c. 1762), Ch'ing dynasty. *Conversation in Autumn,* 1732. Hanging scroll, ink and color on paper. H. 153, W. 39.7 cm (45" × 15⅝"). The Cleveland Museum of Art, Purchase, John L. Severance Fund, **127 left**

Detail of Hua Yen's *Conversation in Autumn,* **127 right**

Li Sung (active c. 1190–1264), Southern Sung dynasty. *The Red Cliff.* Fan painting, ink and color on silk. H. 26, W. 24.8 cm (10¼" × 9¾"). Nelson Gallery-Atkins Museum, Kansas City, Missouri (Nelson Fund), **128**

Wen Cheng-ming (1470–1559), Ming dynasty. *The Red Cliff.* Detail from a hand scroll, ink and color on paper. H. 30.5, L. 141.5 cm (12" × 55¾"). Courtesy of the Smithsonian Institution, Freer Gallery of Art, Washington, D.C., **130**

T'ao Cheng (after 1480–1532), Ming dynasty. Detail, *Chrysanthemums and Cabbages,* dated 1490. Hand scroll, ink and slight color on paper. *Chrysanthemums:* L. 152, W. 28.5 cm (59⅞" × 11¼"). Cleveland Museum of Art, **131 left**

Color wood-block print. H. 26.1, W. 38.3 cm (10¹/₄″ × 15¹/₈″). The Metropolitan Museum of Art, The Howard Mansfield Collection, Rogers Fund, 1936, **246**

Claude Monet (1840–1926), French. *La Japonaise,* 1876. Detail from a painting, oil on canvas. H. 231.1, W. 142.2 cm (91″ × 56″). Courtesy, Museum of Fine Arts, Boston, **247 above left**

Yoshitushi (1838–1892), Meiji period. *Japanese Girl in Western Dress,* 1888. Detail from a color wood-block print. H. 36.3, W. 24.5 cm (14¹/₄″ × 9⁵/₈″). Courtesy of the Art Institute of Chicago, **247 below right**

Giovanni Bellini
Feast of the Gods Italian

Artist Unknown
Horse Race at the Kamo Shrine (detail)

Books for Further Reading

GENERAL

Reischauer, Edwin O., John K. Fairbank, and Albert M. Craig, *A History of East Asian Civilization.* 2 vols, Boston: Houghton Mifflin Co., 1960–1965.

CHINA

Cohen, Joan Lebold, and Jerome Alan Cohen, *China Today and Her Ancient Treasures.* New York: Harry N. Abrams, Inc., 1973.

Dawson, Raymond, *The Legacy of China.* Oxford: The Clarendon Press, 1964.

deBary, Wm. Theodore, Wing-Tsit Chan, Burton Watson, compilers, *Sources of Chinese Tradition.* New York: Columbia University Press, 1960.

Fitzgerald, C. P., *China: A Short Cultural History.* New York: Praeger, 1960. London: The Cresset Press, 1935.

Goodrich, L. Carrington, *A Short History of the Chinese People.* New York: Harper and Row, 1943 (Harper Torchbooks, 1963, 4th edition).

Munro, Eleanor C., *Through the Vermilion Gates: A Journey into China's Past.* New York: Random House, Pantheon Books, 1971.

Schafer, Edward H., *The Golden Peaches of Samarkand.* Berkeley and Los Angeles: University of California Press, 1963.

JAPAN

Castile, Rand. *The Way of Tea.* New York and Tokyo: Weatherhill, 1970.

Keene, Donald, *Language and Portraits, Appreciations of Japanese Culture.* Tokyo and Palo Alto: Kodansha International, Ltd., 1973.

Reischauer, Edwin O., *The Japanese.* Cambridge, Mass.: Harvard University Press, 1977.

Tsunoda, Ryusaku, Wm. Theodore deBary and Donald Keene, compilers. *Sources of Japanese Tradition.* New York: Columbia University Press, 1960.

RELIGION AND PHILOSOPHY

Barrett, William, ed., *D. T. Suzuki, Zen Buddhism: Selected Writings.* New York: Doubleday, 1956 (paperback).

Earhart, H. Byron, *Japanese Religion: Unity and Diversity.* Belmont, California: Dickenson Publishing Co., 1969 (2nd ed. Encino: Cal.: Dickenson Publishing Co., 1974).

Herrigel, Eugene, *Zen in the Art of Archery.* London: Routledge and Kegan Paul, 1953.

Kitagawa, Joseph M., *Religion in Japanese History.* New York and London: Columbia University Press, 1966.

Suzuki, Daisetz, *Zen and Japanese Culture.* London: Routledge and Kegan Paul, 1959.

Waley, Arthur, *Three Ways of Thought in Ancient China.* London: George Allen and Unwin, Ltd., 1939.

————, *The Way and its Power, A Study of the Tao Te Ching and Its Place in Chinese Thought.* London: George Allen and Unwin Ltd., 1939.

Watts, Alan W., *The Way of Zen.* New York: Pantheon Books, a division of Random House, Inc., 1957 (Vintage).

Wright, Arthur F., ed., *The Confucian Persuasion.* Stanford: California: Stanford University Press, 1960.

————, *Buddhism in Chinese History.* Stanford: California: Stanford University Press, 1959.

HISTORY OF ART
General

Fontein, Jan, and Pratapaditya Pal, *Museum of Fine Arts, Boston, Oriental Art.* Distributed by New York Graphic Society. Greenwich, Conn.: 1969.

Freer Gallery of Art, Washington, D.C., *The Freer Gallery of Art.* Vol. 1, *China,* preface by Harold P. Stern. Vol. 2, *Japan,* preface by John A. Pope. Tokyo: Kodansha Ltd., 1971, 1972.

Lee, Sherman E., *A History of Far Eastern Art.* Englewood Cliffs, N.J.: Prentice Hall; and New York: Harry N. Abrams, 1964.

Seckel, Dietrich, *The Art of Buddhism,* trans. by Anne E. Keep. New York: Crown, 1964.

Sullivan, Michael, *Chinese and Japanese Art.* New York: Grolier, Inc., 1965 (Great Art and Artists of the World).

Swann, Peter, *The Art of China, Korea, and Japan.* New York: Frederick A. Praeger, 1963 (paperback).

China

Arts of China. By the editors of Horizon Magazine, New York: American Heritage Publishing Company, Inc., 1969.

Sickman, Laurence, and Alexander Soper. *The Art and Architecture of China.* Baltimore: Penguin Books, 1956.

Sullivan, Michael. *The Arts of China.* (Revised edition of *A Short History of Chinese Art,* first published by Faber and Faber in 1967) London: Thames and Hudson Ltd., 1973. Cardinal edition (paperback) 1973.

Willetts, William, *Foundations of Chinese Art from Neolithic Pottery to Modern Architecture.* New York: McGraw-Hill, 1965.

Japan

Munsterberg, Hugo, *The Arts of Japan.* Tokyo: Rutland, Vermont: Charles E. Tuttle Co., 1956 (paperback).

Paine, Robert Treat, and Alexander Soper, *The Art and Architecture of Japan.* London: Penguin Books, 1955 (2nd edition, 1960, paperback).

Swann, Peter C., *The Art of Japan from the Jomon to the Tokugawa Period.* New York: Crown Publishers, 1960.

Warner, Langdon, *The Enduring Art of Japan.* New York: Grove Press, 1952; Evergreen Books, 1958 (paperback).

Yashiro, Yukio, ed. by Peter Swann, *2,000 Years of Japanese Art.* London: Thames and Hudson, 1958.

ARCHAEOLOGY

Andersson, J. Gunnar, *Children of the Yellow Earth.* London: Kegan Paul, Trench, Trubner and Co., 1934.

The Chinese Exhibition, An Illustrated Handlist of the Exhibition of Archaeological Finds of the People's Republic of China. Washington: National Gallery of Art, 1974; Kansas City: The Nelson Gallery-Atkins Museum, 1975.

Kidder, J. Edward, *Early Japanese Art, the Great Tombs and Treasures.* Princeton, N.J.: D. Van Nostrand Co. Inc., 1964.

Watson, William, *Ancient China, The Discoveries of Post-Liberation Archaeology.* Greenwich, Conn.: New York Graphic Society, 1974.

ARCHITECTURE AND SCULPTURE
China

Boyd, Andrew, *Chinese Architecture and Town Planning,* 1500 B.C.–A.D. 1911. Chicago: University of Chicago Press, 1962.

Sickman, Laurence, and Alexander Soper. *The Art and Architecture of China.* Part II, Architecture. Baltimore: Penguin Books, 1958. Revised edition, paperback, 1971.

Swann, Peter C., *Chinese Monumental Art.* London: Thames and Hudson, 1963.

Wu, Nelson I., *Chinese and Indian Architecture.* London: Prentice-Hall International, 1963 (The Great Ages of World Architecture).

Japan

Alex, William, *Japanese Architecture* (Great Ages of World Architecture Series). New York: Braziller, 1956 (paperback).

Drexler, Arthur, *The Architecture of Japan.* New York: Museum of Modern Art, 1955.

Hayakawa, Masao, *The Garden Art of Japan.* New York and Tokyo: Weatherhill/Heibonsha, 1973.

Tange, Kenzo, *Ise: Prototype of Japanese Architecture.* Cambridge, Mass.: M.I.T. Press, 1965.

———, *Katsura, Tradition and Creation in Japanese Architecture.* New Haven: Yale University Press, 1960.

Warner, Langdon, *The Craft of the Japanese Sculptor.* New York: McFarlane, Warde, McFarlane, and Japan Society of New York, 1936.

Watson, William, *Sculpture of Japan from the Fifth to the Fifteenth Century.* London: The Studio Limited, 1959.

PAINTERS AND PAINTING
China

Bush, Susan, *The Chinese Literati on Painting: Su Shih (1037–1101) to Tung Ch'i-ch'ang (1555–1636).* Cambridge, Mass.: Harvard University Press, 1971.

Cahill, James, *Treasures of Asia—Chinese Painting.* Lausanne: Skira, 1960; also New York: Rizzoli International Publications, Inc., 1977.

Cameron, Alison Stilwell, *Chinese Painting Techniques.* Tokyo: Charles E. Tuttle, 1968.

Chiang, Yee, *The Chinese Eye, An Interpretation of Chinese Painting.* Bloomington: Indiana University Press, 1964 (Midland Book, MB 62).

Edwards, Richard, ed., *The Painting of Tao-chi.* Ann Arbor: University of Michigan, 1967.

———, *The Field of Stones, A Study of the Art of Shen Chou (1427–1509).* Washington: Smithsonian Institution, Freer Gallery of Art, Oriental Studies, No. 5, 1962.

Goepper, Roger, *The Essence of Chinese Painting.* London: Lund Humphries, 1963.

Kuo, Hsi, *An Essay on Landscape Painting,* trans. by Shio Sakanishi. London: J. Murray, 1935.

Lee, Sherman E., *Chinese Landscape Painting.* The Cleveland Museum of Art, 1962 (distributed by Harry N. Abrams, Inc.). New York, 2nd edition.

March, Benjamin, *Some Technical Terms of Chinese Painting.* Baltimore: Waverly Press, Inc., 1935.

Sirén, Osvald, *The Chinese on the Art of Painting.* New York and Hong Kong: Schocken Books, 1963.

Japan

Akiyama, Terukazu, *Treasures of Asia: Japanese Painting.* Lausanne: Skira, 1961.

Covell, Jon Carter, *Under the Seal of Sesshu.* New York: De Pamphilis Press, 1941 (privately printed).

Gray, Basil, *Japanese Screen Painting.* London: Faber and Faber, Limited, 1955.

Grilli, Elise, *The Art of the Japanese Screen.* New York and Tokyo: Weatherhill/Heibonsha, 1973.

———, *Golden Screen Paintings of Japan.* New York: Crown Publishers, Inc., n. d. (Art of the East Library).

———, *Japanese Picture Scrolls.* New York: Crown Publishers, Inc., n. d. (Art of the East Library).

———, trans., Tanio Nakamura, ed., *Sesshu Toyo* (1420–1506) (Kodansha Library of Japanese Art, No. 10). Rutland, Vermont; Tokyo, Japan: Charles E. Tuttle Company, 1957.

Hisamatsu, Shin'ichi, *Zen and the Fine Arts,* transl. by Gishin Tokiwa. Tokyo: Kodansha, 1971.

Lane, Richard, *Masters of the Japanese Print, Their World and Their Work.* Garden City, New York: Doubleday & Company, Inc., 1962.

Lee, Sherman E., *Japanese Decorative Style.* Cleveland: The Cleveland Museum of Art, 1961 (paperback).

Michener, James A., *The Floating World.* New York: Random House, 1954.

Mizuo, Hiroshi, *Edo Painting: Sotatsu and Korin* transl. by John M. Shields. New York and Tokyo: Weatherhill/Heibonsha, 1972.

Seckel, Dietrich, *Emakimono, the Art of the Japanese Painted Handscroll* trans. by J. Maxwell Brownjohn, photographs and foreword by Akihasa Hase. New York: Pantheon Books, 1959.

Sesshu's Long Scroll, A Zen Landscape Journey. Introduction and commentary by Reiko Chiba. Rutland, Vermont and Tokyo: Charles E. Tuttle Company, 1959.

Yonezawa, Yoshiho, and Chu Yoshizawa, *Japanese Painting in the Literati Style* transl. and adapted by Betty Iverson Monroe. New York and Tokyo: Weatherhill/Heibonsha, 1974 (The Heibonsha Survey of Japanese Art, v. 23).

CALLIGRAPHY

Chiang, Yee, *Chinese Calligraphy, An Introduction to its Aesthetic and Technique.* Cambridge, Mass.: Harvard University Press, 3rd edition, 1973.

Driscoll, Lucy, and Kenji Toda, *Chinese Calligraphy.* Chicago: University of Chicago Press: 1935.

Ecke, Tseng Yu-ho, *Chinese Calligraphy.* Philadelphia: Philadelphia Museum of Art, 1971.

Nakata, Yujiro, *The Art of Japanese Calligraphy,* transl. by Alan Woodhull in collaboration with Armins Nikovskis. New York and Tokyo: Weatherhill/Heibonsha, 1973.

CERAMICS

Figgess, John, and Fujio Koyama, *Two Thousand Years of Oriental Ceramics.* New York: Harry N. Abrams, 1960.

Rhodes, Daniel, *Clay and Glazes for the Potter.* New York: Greenberg, 1957; revised edition, Radnor, Pennsylvania: Chilton Book Co., 1973.

China

Beurdeley, Cecile and Michel, *Chinese Ceramics* trans. by Katherine Wilson. New York and London: Harper and Row, 1974.

Garner, Sir Harry, *Oriental Blue and White.* London: Faber and Faber, 1954; 3rd ed., New York and Washington, 1970.

Gompertz, G. St. G. M., *Chinese Celadon Wares.* London: Faber and Faber, 1958.

———, *Celadon Wares.* New York: F. A. Praeger, 1969.

Gray, Basil, *Early Chinese Pottery and Porcelain.* London: Faber and Faber, 1953.

Jenyns, Soame, *Later Chinese Porcelain, The Ch'ing Dynasty* (1644–1912). London: Faber and Faber, 1951.

Valenstein, Suzanne G., *A Handbook of Chinese Ceramics.* New York: The Metropolitan Museum of Art, distributed by the New York Graphic Society, Boston, 1975.

Japan

Jenyns, Soame, *Japanese Porcelain.* London: Faber and Faber, 1965.

———. *Japanese Pottery.* London: Faber and Faber, 1971.

Leach, Bernard. *Kenzan and his Tradition; The Lives and Times of Koetsu, Sotatsu, Korin and Kenzan.* London: Faber and Faber, 1966.

Mikami, Tsugio, *The Art of Japanese Ceramics* trans. by Ann Herring. New York and Tokyo: Weatherhill/Heibonsha, 1972.

Miki, Fumio, *Haniwa* trans. and adapted by Gina Lee Barnes. New York and Tokyo: Weatherhill/Shibundo, 1974.

Miller, Roy Andrew, *Japanese Ceramics,* after the Japanese text by Seiichi Okuda, Fujio Koyama, Seizo Hayashiya and others. Tokyo: Toto Shuppan Co., Ltd.; and Rutland, Vt., and Tokyo: Charles E. Tuttle Co., 1960.

LITERATURE
China

Acker, William, *T'ao the Hermit, Sixty Poems by T'ao Ch'ien.* London and New York: Thames and Hudson, 1952.

Birch, Cyril, ed., *Anthology of Chinese Literature from early times to the fourteenth century.* New York: Grove Press, Inc., 1965 (first Evergreen Edition, 1967).

Bynner, Witter, and Kiang Kang-hu, trans. *The Jade Mountain.* New York: Vintage Books, Random House, 1972 (originally published by Alfred A. Knopf, Inc., 1929).

Watson, Burton, trans, *Cold Mountain, 100 Poems by the T'ang Poet Han-Shan.* New York and London: Columbia University Press, 1970.

Graham, A. C., *Poems of the Late T'ang.* Baltimore: Penguin Books, 1965.

Hawkes, David, *Ch'u Tz'u, the Songs of the South; An Ancient Chinese Anthology.* Oxford: The Clarendon Press, 1959.

Lin Yutang, *The Chinese Theory of Art, Translations from the Masters of Chinese Art.* London: William Heinemann, Ltd., 1967.

———, *The Importance of Understanding.* London: William Heinemann, Ltd., 1960.

Liu, James J. Y., *The Art of Chinese Poetry.* London: Routledge & Kegan Paul; Chicago: The University of Chicago Press, 1962.

Liu, Wu-chi, and Irving Yucheng Lo, eds., *Sunflower Splendor.* Garden City, New York: Anchor Press/Doubleday, 1975 (Anchor Books).

Lu Chi, *The Art of Letters,* trans. by E. R. Hughes. New York: Pantheon, 1951.

Payne, Robert, *The White Pony.* New York: John Day, 1947.

Rexroth, Kenneth, *One Hundred Poems from the Chinese.* New York: New Directions, 1956.

Waley, Arthur, *Chinese Poems.* London: Allen and Unwin, 1946.

———, *Translations from the Chinese.* New York: Vintage Books Edition (a division of Random House), 1971; originally published by Alfred A. Knopf, Inc., 1941.

Watson, Burton, *Early Chinese Literature.* New York: Columbia University Press, 1962.

———, *Su Tung-p'o, Selections from a Sung Dynasty Poet.* New York and London: Columbia University Press, 1965.

Yip, Wai-Lim, ed. and trans., *Chinese Poetry: Major Modes and Genres.* Berkeley: Univeristy of California Press, 1976.

Yoshikawa, Kojiro, *An Introduction to Sung Poetry,* trans. by Burton Watson. Cambridge, Mass.: Harvard University Press, 1967.

Japan

Bownas, Geoffrey, and Anthony Thwaite, trans., *The Penguin Book of Japanese Verse.* Baltimore: Penguin Books, 1964.

Kawabata, Yasunari, *Japan the Beautiful and Myself,* trans. by Edward G. Seidensticker. Tokyo and Palo Alto: Kodansha International Ltd., 1968 (paperback).

Keene, Donald, ed., *Anthology of Japanese Literature from the earliest era to the mid-nineteenth century.* New York: Grove Press, 1955 (first Evergreen Edition, 1960).

———, trans., *Essays in Idleness, the Tsurezuregusa of Kenko.* New York and London: Columbia University Press, 1967. Unesco Collection of Representative Works, Japanese Series.

————, *Japanese Literature, an Introduction for Western Readers*. New York: Grove Press, 1955.

The Manyoshu, the Nippon Gakujutsu Shinkokai Translation of One Thousand Poems, with a foreword by Donald Keene. New York and London: Columbia University Press, 1965. Unesco Collection of Representative Works, Japanese Series.

McCullough, Helen Craig, *Tales of Ise, Lyrical Episodes from Tenth-Century Japan.* Stanford, Cal.: Stanford University Press, 1968.

Morris, Ivan, trans. and ed., *The Pillow Book of Sei Shonagon.* 2 vol. New York: Columbia University Press, 1967.

————, *The World of the Shining Prince.* New York: Alfred A. Knopf, 1969.

Murasaki, Lady, *The Tale of Genji,* trans. by Arthur Waley. 6 vol. London: G. Allen and Unwin, 1926–33.

Murasaki Shikibu, *The Tale of Genji,* trans. by Edward G. Seidensticker. 2 vol. New York: Alfred A. Knopf, 1976.

MEETING OF EAST AND WEST

Crossman, Carl L., *The China Trade, Export Paintings, Furniture, Silver and Other Objects.* Princeton: The Pyne Press, 1972.

Honour, Hugh. *Chinoiserie, the Vision of Cathay.* London: John Murray, 1961.

Ives, Colta Feller, *The Great Wave: The Influence of Japanese Woodcuts on French Prints.* New York: The Metropolitan Museum of Art, 1974 (distributed by the New York Graphic Society).

Pineau, Roger, ed., *The Japan Expedition, 1853–1854: The Personal Journal of Commodore Mathew C. Perry.* Washington, D. C.: Smithsonian Institution, 1968.

Rowland, Benjamin, Jr., *Art in East and West, An Introduction through Comparisons.* Cambridge, Mass.: Harvard University Press, 1954.

Sansom, George B., *The Western World and Japan, A Study in the Interaction of European and Asiatic Cultures.* New York: Alfred A. Knopf, 1950 (Vintage V-867).

Sullivan, Michael, *The Meeting of Eastern and Western Art from the Sixteenth Century to the Present Day.* London: Thames and Hudson, 1973.

Weisberg, Gabriel P., ed., *Japonisme, Japanese Influence on French Art, 1854–1910.* Cleveland: The Cleveland Museum of Art, The Rutgers University Art Gallery, and The Walters Art Gallery, 1975.

Yamada, Chisaburo F., general editor, *Dialogue in Art, Japan and the West.* Tokyo, New York and San Francisco: Kodansha International Ltd., 1976.

Chronology

CHINA

Neolithic Times	c. 7000——		Yuan	1279–1368
Dynasties			Ming	1368–1644
Shang (shang as in gong)	c. 1750–1111 B.C.*		Ch'ing	1644–1912
Chou	1111–221			
Ch'in	221–206			
Han	B.C. 206–A.D. 220			

Shang (shang as in gong) c. 1750–1111 B.C.*
Chou 1111–221
Ch'in 221–206
Han B.C. 206–A.D. 220
Six Dynasties 220–589
Sui 581–618
T'ang 618–907
Five Dynasties 907–960
Sung 960–1279
  Northern Sung Dynasty
  A.D. 960–1127
  Southern Sung Dynasty
  A.D. 1127–1279

Yuan 1279–1368
Ming 1368–1644
Ch'ing 1644–1912

*According to the chronology of Tung Tso-pien

Rhyme for Remembering Dynasties
(This simplified jingle may help you keep the chronology straight.)

Shang, Chou, Han
Six, Sui, T'ang
Five, Sung, Yuan
Ming, and Ch'ing.

JAPAN

Jomon ?–c. 300 B.C.
Yayoi c. 300 B.C.–A.D. 300
Kofun (Tumulus) c. 300–552
Asuka Period
  (Suiko) 538–645
Nara Period 645–794
  Early Nara (Hakuho)
  Period 645–710
  Late Nara (Tempyo)
  Period 710–794
Heian Period 794–1185
  Early Heian
  (Jogan) Period 794–897

Late Heian
  (Fujiwara)
  Period 897–1185
Kamakura Period 1185–1334
Namboku-cho
  Period 1334–1392
Muromachi (Ashikaga)
  Period 1334–1573
Momoyama Period 1573–1615
Edo (Tokugawa)
  Period 1615–1868
  Early Edo Period 1615–1716
  Late Edo Period 1716–1868
Modern Japan 1868–to date

Hints on Pronunciation

CHINESE

Various ways have been tried for writing down in our alphabet the sound of Chinese as pronounced in the official language, Mandarin, the speech of Peking. The method still generally used is called the Wade–Giles System although a new method has been devised by the People's Republic of China.

Vowels and Vowel Combinations

a	as in f*a*ther	*ai*	as in *ai*sle
e	as in stol*e*n	*au*	as in s*au*erkr*au*t
i	as in mach*i*ne	*ei*	as in w*ei*gh
o	as in J*o*seph,	*ou*	as in b*ou*lder
	sometimes like *o* in s*o*ft		
u	as in r*u*mor	*ang*	like *ahng* or *ong* in many words
ü	like the *u* of German,	*ung*	like *oong*
	or the French *u*	*ih*	like *ir* sound in st*ir*

Consonants

ch'	as in *ch*ug	*t'*	as in *t*in
ch	as in *j*ug	*t*	as in *d*in
k'	as in *c*ame	*ts'*	as in *ts*way
k	as in *g*ame	*ts*	as in *ds*way
p'	as in *p*in	*j*	is almost the English *r* (jen-run)
p	as in *b*in		

JAPANESE

The pronunciation of Japanese as it is written in our alphabet is much simpler than Chinese. It is usually said that the vowels are pronounced as in Italian, the consonants as in English. In dipthongs, the sounds of both vowels are heard. G is always hard as in "get" or in "Genji." In words of more than one syllable "u" is slurred over, as in "netsuke." A final "u," as in the name "Sotatsu" is scarcely heard.

Glossary

ALBUM LEAF. A small painting complete in itself, rectangular, or rounded when intended for a fan. After the fourteenth century, such paintings were often gathered in portfolios, usually as a consecutive series of paintings.

AMITABHA (Japanese, AMIDA) BUDDHA. Amitabha was the name given to the Buddha who rules the Western Paradise, worshipped by followers of the Pure Land sect. He was a symbol of compassion, welcoming to his paradise all who in sincerity called on his name.

BODHIDHARMA (Japanese, DARUMA). Indian monk who traditionally came to China in A.D. 520 and founded the Ch'an sect of Buddhism.

BODHISATTVA (Japanese, BOSATSU). One who has attained enlightenment but gives up *nirvana,* or salvation, in order to aid all suffering beings.

BUDDHA (Japanese, BUTSU). Buddha means "the awakened" or "enlightened one." It was believed that the historical Buddha, a prince of the Shakya tribe born in the north of India in the sixth century B.C., was only one of many manifestations of the Buddha.

BYOBU. Japanese folding screens. These decorative and functional screens, sometimes single, more often paired, served as the support for important paintings by master artists.

CALLIGRAPHY. The art of beautiful handwriting.

CELADON. A European term to describe various Far Eastern ceramic wares with gray-green or blue-green glazes, including the celebrated imperial porcelains of the Sung dynasty in China.

CERAMICS. Objects of fired clay: earthenware, stoneware, porcellaneous stoneware, or porcelain. Pottery is also an inclusive term for all objects of fired clay.

CH'AN (Japanese, ZEN) BUDDHISM. Ch'an monks believed in seeking enlightenment without dependence upon scriptures or ceremony. Introduced into Japan in the thirteenth century, Zen has influenced much that we think of as characteristically Japanese.

CHINOISERIES. A French word for adaptations of Chinese styles in European art. The fashion for chinoiseries was at its height in the eighteenth century.

COLOPHON. There may be inscriptions on a Chinese painting but a colophon, in the case of a hand scroll, follows the actual painting. These comments, in prose or verse—by contemporaries of the artist, or written at a later time—often provide information about the painting, subsequent owners, and connoisseurs.

CRACKLE. In ceramics, crackle refers to the network of tiny cracks in a glaze; such cracks probably occurred first as an accident of the firing and were then later consciously controlled.

DAIMYO. Feudal lords of provinces in Japan.

DARUMA. *See* BODHIDHARMA.

DYNASTY. In China a dynasty refers to a royal house that chooses a name for itself. *Ch'ing,* for example, means "bright" or "shining" and was chosen by the Manchu rulers of China as a dynastic name (1644–1911).

EDO. An earlier name for Tokyo and the name given to the period, 1615–1867, sometimes called Tokugawa for the family name of the ruling shoguns.

EMAKIMONO (Japanese). *See* HAND SCROLL.

FUJIWARA. Ruling family of the late Heian period in Japan.

FUSUMA (Japanese). Sliding panels of thick paper over wooden frames used as movable walls in houses, temples, or other buildings, often decorated with paintings or calligraphy.

GLAZE. A glossy finish, coating the surface of a ceramic piece.

HABOKU. Japanese word for the "flung ink" technique of monochrome ink painting.

HAIKU. A term invented in nineteenth-century Japan to designate a poem complete in seventeen syllables arranged in a pattern of 5-7-5, and the most popular poetic form in Japan since the latter part of the seventeenth century.

HAND SCROLL (Japanese, EMAKIMONO). A horizontal painting, mounted on silk or paper to be slowly unrolled from right to left. Hand scrolls vary greatly in length and were never displayed fully open.

HANGING SCROLL (Japanese, KAKEMONO). A painting in the vertical format intended for hanging on a wall. Rolled up and tied with its neat string, it could be conveniently stored.

HANIWA ("ring of clay"). Clay cylinders, often figurative, placed around the perimeter of ancient Japanese burial mounds.

JADE. An English term used to describe two stones, somewhat similar in appearance but differing in composition—both extremely hard and capable of high polish. The more precious—nephrite jade—has been worked with extraordinary skill since ancient times in China. Jadeite jade appeared much later and is more familiar in the West. Magical and symbolic properties have long been attributed to jade. And jade is not always green. As a Chinese once wrote: "There are many different colors, among which snow white, kingfisher green, beeswax yellow, cinnabar red and ink black are considered valuable; but the most difficult to find are pieces of pure mutton-fat texture with vermilion spots, and others of bright spinach green flecked with shining points of gold."

JAPONISME. A movement in French painting, printmaking, and the decorative arts that reflected influences from Japan in the second half of the nineteenth century and into the first years of the twentieth.

JODO. Japanese name for the Pure Land sect of Buddhism, teaching that salvation lies in calling on the name of Amida Buddha.

KAKEMONO. *See* HANGING SCROLL.

KANNON. *See* KUAN YIN.

KANO. A school of Japanese painting founded in the fifteenth century by the father of Kano Motonobu (1476–1559) and still flourishing in the nineteenth century. Hereditary members all used the family name, such as Kano Eitoku, Kano Sanraku, Kano Tanyu.

KUAN YIN (Japanese, KANNON). The Bodhisattva of infinite compassion, originally masculine, later represented as the feminine goddess of mercy.

LACQUER. A varnish made from the sap of a special tree in China and Japan, used to give a smooth hard finish to such materials as wood, leather, metal, or silk. The craft of lacquer required extraordinary skill and patience, whether the results were subtle or sumptuous. In itself a preservative, lacquer was applied in many layers and could be carved, decorated, or used as a painting medium.

LITERATI. The Latin term for scholars, or men of letters, and the accepted translation of the Chinese phrase "wen-jen" (*bunjinga* in Japanese).

MAITREYA (Japanese, MIROKU). The Buddha of the Future, a sort of Messiah, sometimes designated as a Bodhisattva.

MING-CH'I. Objects placed in the tomb in China, often of clay, glazed or unglazed, especially models of human figures, animals, buildings, utensils—providing necessities or luxuries for the afterlife.

MIROKU. *See* MAITREYA.

MONOGATARI. Romance or narrative prose in Japan—The Ise monogatari, Genji monogatari, Heike monogatari, etc.

MONO NO AWARE. A Japanese phrase variously translated as "the pity of things," "sensitivity to things," "the blending of elegance and pathos." It is the association of beauty and sorrow, the recognition of the transiency of all life.

NANGA. Another Japanese name for the group known as *bunjinga*. *See* LITERATI.

NEMBUTSU (Japanese). Repetition of the name of a Buddha, especially the name of Amida Buddha who rules the Western Paradise.

NIRVANA. A Buddhist term—release from the desires and sufferings of this world and from being born again here. Salvation is another translation.

NO. The classic, aristocratic drama of Japan.

PI. A jade disc pierced in the center with a circular hole—a ritual object in ancient China.

PORCELAIN. By Chinese definition, "a ware in which glaze coalesces with the body, and which when struck with a hard instrument produces a clear, resonant tone." It is made of a white china clay, "kaolin," usually with some feldspar and flint. It is hard, dense, impervious to liquids, and may be translucent when thinly potted.

RAIGO. The descent of Amida Buddha with heavenly beings to welcome the soul of the dying believer into his Western Paradise.

RENGA. The Japanese art of linked verse.

RIMPA. The decorative school of the seventeenth, eighteenth, and nineteenth centuries in Japan, founded by Sotatsu, sometimes called the Sotatsu-Korin School.

SAMURAI. A warrior in Japanese feudal days.

SATORI. The moment of insight or of enlightenment in Zen Buddhism.

SEAL. Chinese and Japanese paintings are usually stamped in a soft red with the seal of the artist, or of his studio, or with the seal of an owner or an admirer of the painting. Made of various materials, such as ivory, jade, stone, and wood, the carving of seals was regarded as a fine art.

SHINGON (Chinese CHEN-YEN). The "True Word" sect of Buddhism, brought back to Japan from China by Kobo Daishi (774–855).

SHINTO. The early animistic beliefs of the Japanese people that have survived alongside of Buddhism and have contributed to their attitudes toward nature, their love of beauty, and their respect for the imperial family.

SHOGUN. A military dictator and head of government in Japan from the Kamakura through the Edo period.

STONEWARE. Vitrified, high-fired pottery made of stoneware clay with the addition of some other materials. It is dense, hard, and impervious to liquid.

SUIBOKU ("water and ink"). The important school of painting in Japan introduced from China in the Muromachi period—paintings in ink, sometimes with washes of light color.

SUMI-E. Painting in ink. It represents the influence of Chinese ink painting upon Japanese art, as opposed to YAMATO-E, painting in the Japanese taste.

TAO. Tao means "the Way," and Taoism is a Chinese philosophy or religion related to the spirit or principle of nature.

T'AO-T'IEH. An important element in the decoration of ancient Chinese bronzes, a masklike head that may suggest a tiger, bull, or ogre. It looks out at us with round staring eyes, with horns and fangs.

TEA-TASTE. Zen ideas infused Japanese culture in the fifteenth and sixteenth centuries through the influence of the tea masters. Their taste as expressed in the tea ceremony was for the understated, the rustic, and the apparently careless. Three untranslatable words are used to describe tea-taste: *shibui* (astringent), *wabi* (solitary, remote), and *sabi* (worn, antique).

TENDAI (Chinese, T'IEN-T'AI). The "Heavenly Terrace" sect within Buddhism, introduced into Japan in A.D. 805 and the most powerful sect in Lady Murasaki's time.

TOKONOMA. An alcove in a Japanese house for the display of a KAKEMONO (painting or calligraphy), along with a simple flower arrangement or *objet d'art*.

TOKUGAWA. Name of the family of shoguns who ruled Japan from the beginning of the seventeenth century until 1867. *See* EDO.

TORII. The two-pillar gateway to a Shinto shrine.

TS'UN. "Texture wrinkles" made with brush and ink. In Chinese painting after a form has been outlined—rock, mountain, tree trunk, etc.—it may be given a specific character by the use of *ts'un*. Many types are differentiated as "hemp-fiber *ts'un*," "raindrop *ts'un*," "ax-cut *ts'un*" (both large and small), "nail-extracted-from-mud *ts'un*," and so on.

UKIYO-E. "Picture of the floating world," of the fleeting world, paintings and wood-block prints of genre subjects, especially the pleasure quarters and theatre world of Edo period, Japan.

VAIROCANA. The primordial Buddha, the original spiritual source of the whole cosmos.

WAKA. The classic Japanese verse form of thirty-one syllables, commonly called *tanka* (short poems) in recent years.

YAMATO. The ancient name of Japan, applied to the region around Nara, Osaka, and Kyoto, the center of early cultural and historical developments.

YAMATO-E. A style of painting developed in the Heian period reflecting purely Japanese taste in color and in subject matter.

ZEN. *See* CH'AN BUDDHISM.

Index

(Page numbers in italics refer to illustrations.)

About the Author

Janet Gaylord Moore has always been deeply involved with art, as educator, curator, artist, and writer. Her book, THE MANY WAYS OF SEEING: *An Introduction to the Pleasures of Art*, written for older children as well as for adults, was a Newbery Honor Book. A graduate of Vassar College, Ms. Moore studied painting in France, Italy, and at the Art Students' League in New York. She lived for a time in Peking, and traveled extensively in other parts of China as well as in Japan, and her interest in the arts and culture of these two countries has been a lifelong one.

Ms. Moore taught art at the Laurel School in Shaker Heights before joining the staff of the Cleveland Museum of Art, an institution which has one of the finest collections of Oriental art in the United States. In her work there as an Associate Curator in the Education Department, she observed that many people, even those who were well-informed about Western and European art, were confused by the various styles and periods of Eastern art, and often, therefore, failed to appreciate and enjoy some of the great works of Eastern art to the fullest. She came to realize that there was a vast need for information about the historical and social background, the religions, and the literature of China and Japan, as well as about the art and the artists themselves. The present volume grew out of this observation.

Ms. Moore recently retired from her post at the Cleveland Museum of Art in order to devote more time to her own writing and painting. She now lives in a small town on the coast of Maine, in a house on a rocky promontory with an unimpeded and inspiring view of the Atlantic Ocean.

The text type is Palatino and the display type is Goudy Old Style.
The color art was separated and printed by Federated Lithographers.
The text and black and white art was printed by Halliday Lithograph Corp.
Bound by The Book Press.
Designed by Sallie Baldwin of Bob Antler & Sallie Baldwin, Inc.